REF

PE
1693
M48
1988

Miller, Stuart W.

Concise dictionary of
acronyms and
initialisms.

$22.95

DATE			

© THE BAKER & TAYLOR CO.

Concise

Dictionary

OF
Acronyms

AND
Initialisms

SHAW UNIVERSITY LIBRARY
118 E. SOUTH ST.
RALEIGH, NC 27611

Concise

Dictionary

OF
Acronyms

AND
Initialisms

Stuart W. Miller

James E. Cheek
Learning Resources Center

92-2688

SHAW UNIVERSITY LIBRARY
118 E. SOUTH ST.
RALEIGH, NC 27611

Facts On File Publications
New York, New York • Oxford, England

REF
PE
1693
M48
1988

Concise Dictionary of Acronyms and Initialisms

Copyright © 1988 by Stuart W. Miller

All rights reserved. No part of this book may
be reproduced or utilized in any form or by any
means, electronic or mechanical, including
photocopying, recording, or by any information
storage and retrieval systems, without permission
in writing from the publisher.

Library of Congress Cataloging-in-Publication Data

Miller, Stuart W.
    Concise dictionary of acronyms and initialisms / by Stuart W. Miller
        p.   cm.
    ISBN 0-8160-1577-5 : $29.95
    1. Acronyms—Dictionaries.   I. Title.
PE1693.M48   1988
423'.1—dc19   87-30468
                                                                    CIP

Interior Design by Ron Monteleone

British CIP data available on request

Printed in the United States of America

10 9 8 7 6 5 4 3 2

To Richard P. Miller
1922-1985

INTRODUCTION

In 1985, as chairman of the *Reference Books Bulletin* Editorial Board, I organized a meeting at the American Library Association Annual Conference in Chicago at which reference book publishers and librarians were brought together in an informal forum to exchange ideas about needed reference works. A rather lively interchange occurred and one idea that met with warm approval among the librarians was the concept of an abridged dictionary of acronyms.

The librarians at this meeting all acknowledged the value of the major existing tool in this area—Gale Research Company's *Acronyms, Initialisms & Abbreviations Dictionary*. At the same time, there appeared to be a belief that this work was almost *too* exhaustive for many general library situations. It contains thousands of acronyms from specialized fields and what are surely nonce terms—none of which seems likely to be known or encountered by anyone not a specialist in the given field or situation. Further thought suggested that a shorter work, incorporating only the more common acronyms, initialisms, and abbreviations might find a place in a nontechnical library reference collection and be useful in a personal reference collection as well. The result is this volume. It in no way should be seen as a substitute for more comprehensive works or for those works covering a particular field.

This work attempts to identify those acronyms, initialisms, and abbreviations that would appear in a newspaper, news magazine, or other general publication; be encountered by an individual in the regular course of events; and/or be found as a clue or an answer in a crossword puzzle. Inevitably, such criteria demand judgment on the part of the compiler and some users will not agree that some of the selections are justified; other users will not find what they expect. To elaborate somewhat, my goal was to produce a book of manageable size, reasonable cost, and basic utility. The results may therefore be best described as a "barebones" dictionary, intended for ready-reference situations.

Since I hope that many librarians will use this work, I have, for their convenience, included items from the library and publishing fields (although the more esoteric items were eliminated).

Order in this work is letter by letter, ignoring punctuation and/or spacing. Any entries incorporating a number or symbol follow immediately after the listings for that alphabetical sequence. Identical acronyms appear alphabetically by their full expressions. Other than simply saying what it means, I have added clarifying remarks when it seemed useful or necessary for full comprehension. I have excluded plural forms. When the use of any item might, in some circumstances, be considered derogatory or otherwise offensive, the fact is so noted. No approval of such usage should be inferred from the inclusion of these possibly offensive terms.

I would like to acknowledge those unknown librarians at that 1985 meeting who gave me the idea for this book in the first place. In addition, the staff of Facts On File (Ed Knappman especially) has been most supportive and patient with this dilatory author. Thanks are also extended to Peggy Sullivan, Dean of the College of Professional Studies, Northern Illinois University, for getting me involved in reference book publishing in the first place. My colleagues and friends on the *Reference Books Bulletin* Editorial Board from 1980-1985 taught me a great deal about reference works and I deeply appreciated the opportunity to serve as chair of that group for three years. Helen K. Wright of the American Library Association helped to teach me too and imparted her very high standards for the reference book publishing community to me. I hope this work comes up to *her* mark. Needless to say, any errors are my responsibility.

Charles LaGrutta who, unasked, took on the job of feeding and generally putting up with this madly typing author in the last throes of creation, deserves special recognition. He endured with great equanimity.

I dedicate this book to my father. As a good scientist, he always believed in exactitude, the best possible use of one's resources, and finishing one's projects. He applied those beliefs regardless of whether he was conducting an experiment in his lab or hanging wallpaper at home. As a good man, he accepted people for who they were and what they could do. As a good father, he would have had nothing but praise for this book. After all, it was his son who was the author. I can only hope this book meets the standards he always set for himself.

Stuart W. Miller
Chicago, Illinois

A

A	Alto
Å	Angstrom (measure of light; one ten-billionth of a meter)
A	*Anno* (Latin: "year")
A	April
a	Are (100 square meters)
A	Association
A	August
A	First class discounted (airfare)
A	Shoe width for a woman's size (up to AAAAA, the narrowest)
A1	First-class; high quality
1-A	Draft classification; eligible for induction

3-A	Draft classification; not eligible because of hardships to dependents
4-A	Draft classification; veteran status
A-levels	British college entrance exams
AA	Academy Award (Oscar)
AA	Affirmative action
AA	Alcoholics Anonymous
AA	Aluminum Co. of America
AA	American Airlines
AA	Automobile Association (of Great Britain)
aa	Equal amounts of each (prescription note)
Aa	Moody's bond rating: high
AA	Standard & Poor's bond rating: high
AA	Shoe width for a woman's size
AAA	Agricultural Adjustment Act/Administration/Agency (New Deal farm programs and agencies)
AAA	Amateur Athletic Association (of Great Britain)
AAA	American Automobile Association ("Triple A"; motorists' organization)
Aaa	Moody's bond rating: highest

AAA	Shoe width for a woman's size
AAA	Standard & Poor's bond rating: highest
AAAA	Shoe width for a woman's size
AAAAA	Shoe width for a woman's size (narrowest)
AAAL	American Academy of Arts and Letters
AAAS	American Association for the Advancement of Science
AALL	American Association of Law Libraries
AAP	Association of American Publishers
AARP	American Association of Retired Persons
AAUP	American Association of University Professors (union)
AB	Air Base
AB	Alberta (U.S. postal code)
AB	Assembly bill (in U.S. state legislatures, the lower house)
AB	Bachelor of Arts (academic degree; see also BA)
ABA	American Bankers Association
ABA	American Bar Association
ABA	American Basketball Association (later NBA; see below)

ABA	American Book Awards
ABA	American Booksellers Association
ABC	American Broadcasting Companies (radio and television network)
abl.	Ablative
ABM	Antiballistic missile
ABS	American Bible Society
ABSCAM	FBI operation of 1979 to entice U.S. officials to take bribes, said to be named after "Arab Scam" and other variants thereon
ABT	American Ballet Theater
ABTA	Association of British Travel Agents
a/c	Account (British)
Ac	Actinium (element)
AC	Air conditioning
AC	Alternating current
AC	American Can Company
Acad.	Academy
ACAS	Advisory Conciliation & Arbitration Service (of Great Britain)
acc.	Accusative

acct.	Accountant/Account
AC/DC	Bisexual
ACE	Army Corps of Engineers (U.S.)
ACLU	American Civil Liberties Union
ACM	Advanced cruise missile
ACORN	Association of Community Organizations for Reform Now
ACRS	Accelerated cost recovery system (refers to depreciation rules for U.S. income taxes)
ACS	American College of Surgeons
act.	Active
ACT	Automatic credit transfer
ACTWU	Amalgamated Clothing and Textile Workers Union
AD	*Anno Domini* (Latin: "the year of our Lord")
ADA	American Dental Association
ADA	Americans for Democratic Action (liberal lobbying group)
ADC	Aid to Dependent Children (welfare program; see also AFDC below)
ADC	Aide-de-camp (usually a military term)

adj.	Adjective
Adj.	Adjutant
ad lib	*ad libitum* (Latin: "as desired"; extemporaneous)
admin.	Administration/Administrator
ADT	Atlantic Daylight Time
ADT	Automatic debit transfer
adv.	Adverb
advt.	Advertisement
AE	American Express (credit card or company)
AEC	Atomic Energy Commission (defunct; see NRC below)
AEF	American Expeditionary Force (U.S. military forces in Europe in World War I)
AEI	American Enterprise Institute (conservative think tank)
AEP	American Electric Power Company, Inc.
AFAA	Airline Flight Attendants Association (union)
AFB	Air Force base
AFC	Air Force Cross (British military decoration)

AFDC	Aid to Families with Dependent Children (welfare program; see also ADC above)
AFI	American Film Institute
AFL	American Federation of Labor (coalition of craft unions)
AFL	American Football League
AFL-CIO	American Federation of Labor-Congress of Industrial Organizations (coalition of craft and industrial unions; see also AFL above and CIO below)
AFM	Air Force Medal (British military decoration)
AFN	Armed Forces Network (U.S.)
AFP	American Federation of Police
AFS	American Field Service (see AFSIIP)
AFSC	American Friends' Service Committee (Quaker relief organization)
AFSCME	American Federation of State, County and Municipal Employees (union)
AFSIIP	AFS International-Intercultural Programs (group organizing exchange programs with foreign countries)
AFT	American Federation of Teachers (union)
AFT	American Film Theater

AFTRA	American Federation of Television and Radio Artists (union)
Ag	Argentum (element, silver)
AG	Attorney General (for both the U.S. federal and state governments)
Ag.	August
AGI	Adjusted gross income
AGM	Annual general meeting (British)
AGMA	American Guild of Musical Artists (union)
AGO	Attorney General's Opinion (federal or state-level advisory on legal questions; do not have force of law)
AHA	American Heart Association
AHL	American Hockey League
AIA	American Institute of Architects
AID	Agency for International Development (U.S. agency administering foreign aid programs)
AID	Artificial insemination by donor
AIDS	Acquired immune deficiency syndrome
AIM	Accuracy in Media (watchdog group policing news reports)
AK	Alaska (U.S. postal code)

aka	Also known as
AKC	American Kennel Club
AL	Alabama (U.S. postal code)
Al	Aluminum (element)
AL	American League (baseball teams)
AL	*American Libraries* (publication)
ALA	American Library Association
ALCAN	Alaska-Canada (highway)
ALCOA	Aluminum Co. of America
ALD	Allied-Signal Inc.
alt.	Alternate/alternative
alt.	Altitude
Am.	American
Am.	Amos (book of the Bible)
AM	Amplitude modulation (broadcasting system)
AM	*Ante meridiem* (Latin: "being before noon")
A & M	Ancient and modern hymns
AMA	American Medical Association

AMB	American Brands, Inc.
AMC	American Motors Corporation
Amer.	American
Amerind	American Indian
AMEX	American Express Co.
AMEX	American Stock Exchange
AMI	Alternative mortgage index
AMR	AMR Corporation (formerly American Airlines)
Amoco	"American Oil Co." (AMOCO now the name of what was formerly Standard Oil Company [Indiana])
Amtrak	American Track (popular name for the National Railroad Passenger Corporation, U.S. agency providing passenger rail service)
ANC	African National Congress
ANC	Anchorage, Alaska airport
ANSI	American National Standards Institute (U.S. agency developing standards for various procedures, undertakings, etc.)
ant.	Anterior
ant.	Antonym

ANTA	American National Theater Academy (defunct)
ANZAC	Australia-New Zealand Army Corps (or a person serving therein)
ANZUS	Australia-New Zealand-United States
Ap.	April
AP	Associated Press (news service)
A & P	Great Atlantic & Pacific Tea Company (grocery chain)
APB	All points bulletin (police broadcast)
Apl.	April
APO	Army (or Air Force) Post Office
app.	Appendix
Apr.	April
aq.	Water (prescription note)
AR	Annual return (British)
Ar	Argon (element)
AR	Arkansas (U.S. postal code)
ARA	Automatic Retailers of America (acronym now official name)
ARAMCO	Arabian-American Oil Co.

ARC	AIDS-related complex
ARCO	Atlantic Richfield Co.
ARIBA	Associate of the Royal Institute of British Architects
ARM	Adjustable rate mortgage
art.	Article
ARV	AIDS-associated retrovirus
ARVN	Army of the Republic of Vietnam (South Vietnamese army; defunct)
A-S	Air shuttle
AS	American Samoa (U.S. postal code)
As	Arsenic (element)
ASA	Amateur Swimming Association (of Great Britain)
ASA	American Standards Association (now ANSI, see above; previously seen preceding film speed on film rolls; ISO [see below] now used)
ASAP	As soon as possible
ASB	Alternative Book Service (Anglican/ Episcopal liturgical guide)
ASCAP	American Society of Composers, Authors, and Publishers (union)

ASPCA	American Society for the Prevention of Cruelty to Animals
Assn.	Association
Assoc.	Associate
Assoc.	Association
AST	Atlantic Standard Time
ASV	American Standard Version (of the Bible)
At	Astatine (element)
ATC	Air Training Corps (Great Britain)
ATL	Atlanta, Georgia airport
Atl.	Atlantic
ATM	Automated/automatic teller machine
ATT	American Telephone & Telegraph Company
AT & T	American Telephone & Telegraph Company
atty.	Attorney
ATV	All terrain vehicle
Au.	August
Au	Aurum (element, gold)
Aug.	August

AV	Audiovisual
AV	Authorized Version (of the Bible; also known as the King James' Version or KJV)
AVDP	*Avoirdupois* (French: literally, "property by weight"; refers to weights and measures system based on 16 ounces to a pound and an ounce of 16 drams)
Ave.	Avenue
avg.	Average
AWACS	Advanced or airborne warning and control system
AWOL	Absent without leave (U.S. military)
AXP	American Express Co.
AZ	Arizona (U.S. postal code)

B

B	Baritone
B	Bass(o)
B	Boron (element)
B	Breakfast
B	Coach economy discounted (airfare)
BA	Bachelor of Arts (academic degree; see also AB)
Ba	Barium (element)
BA	Boeing Company
BA	British Airways (see also BEA and BOAC)
BAA	British Airports Authority
BAM	Brooklyn Academy of Music (Brooklyn, New York)
BAOR	British Army of the Rhine

Bart.	Baronet (British title)
BART	Bay Area Rapid Transit (San Francisco, California area)
BASIC	Beginners' All-Purpose Symbolic Instruction Code (computer language)
BAT	British-American Tobacco Co.
BB	Shot pellet
B & B	Bed and breakfast (type of lodging facility)
B & B	Brandy and benedictine
BBB	Better Business Bureau
BBC	British Broadcasting Corporation
BBL	Barrel
BBQ	Barbecue
BC	Before Christ
BC	British Columbia (Canadian province, U.S. postal code)
BC	Bureau of the Census (U.S. agency; major statistics-gathering office)
B & C	Biopsy and curettage (medical procedure)
BCA	Boys' Clubs of America
bcc	Blind carbon copy

BCP	*Book of Common Prayer* (Anglican/ Episcopal service book)
BCR	Bibliographical Center for Research (library network)
Bd.	Board
BDRM	Bedroom
Be	Beryllium (element)
BEA	British European Airways (merged with BOAC [see below] to form BA [see above])
BEd.	Bachelor of Education (academic degree)
BEF	British Expeditionary Force (military forces overseas in both World Wars)
BEM	British Empire Medal (honor)
BENELUX	Belgium, Netherlands, and Luxembourg
BFA	Bachelor of Fine Arts (academic degree)
BFPO	British Forces Post Office
BGA	Better Government Association
Bi	Bismuth (element)
b.i.d.	Twice a day (prescription note)
BIP	*Books in Print* (publication)
Bk	Berkelium (element)

bk.	Book
BKL	Cleveland, Ohio airport (Burke)
BLM	Bureau of Land Management (U.S. agency controlling non-park land of the U.S. Dept. of the Interior)
BLS	Bureau of Labor Statistics (U.S. agency gathering consumer and labor-related statistics)
BLT	Bacon, lettuce, and tomato sandwich
Blvd.	Boulevard
BM	British Museum
BMA	British Medical Association
BMOC	Big man on campus
BMW	Name for cars produced by the German company Bayerische Motoren Werke (Bavarian Motor Works)
BN	Braniff Airways
BNI	Burlington Northern Inc.
BNOC	British National Oil Corporation
BO	Body odor
BOAC	British Overseas Airways Corporation (merged with BEA [see above] to form BA [see above])

B of E	Bank of England
Bohunk	Bohemian-Hungarian (now generally considered a derogatory term)
BOMC	Book of the Month Club (mail order book club)
BOS	Boston, Massachusetts airport
BOS	Boston Stock Exchange
BOT	Board of Trade (generic; usually preceded by specific identifier; see, e.g., CBOT)
BP	Blood pressure
BP	Boiling point
BP	British Petroleum
BPI	*Business Periodicals Index* (publication)
BPOE	Benevolent and Protective Order of Elks (fraternal organization)
BR	Bedroom
BR	British Railways
Br	Bromine (element)
Brit.	British/Britain
bro.	Brother

BRS	Bibliographic Retrieval Services (vendor of computer-based information sources)
BS	Bachelor of Science (academic degree)
BS	Bethlehem Steel Corporation
BSA	Boy Scouts of America
BSc.	Bachelor of Science (academic degree)
BSI	British Standards Institute
BST	British Summer Time
Bt.	Baronet (British title)
BT	British Telecom
BTA	Board of Tax Appeals (generic for a government agency)
BTA	British Travel Authority
BTU	British thermal unit
Bty	Battery
bu	Bushel
BUF	Buffalo, New York airport
BVD	Underwear (Bradley, Voorhies, and Day, founders of company manufacturing mens' underwear; now, sometimes used as a generic term)

BVM	Blessed Virgin Mary
B/W	Black and white
BWI	Baltimore, Maryland airport
BYOB	Bring your own bottle/booze

C

C	Average
C	Calorie
C	Carbon (element)
C	Centigrade
c	Copyright
c	Cup (measure)
C	One hundred (Roman numeral)
C	Shoe width for a man's size (medium narrow)
C	Shoe width for a woman's size (medium wide)
Ca	Calcium (element)
CA	California (U.S. postal code)
C/A	Central air (conditioning)

ca.	*Circa* (Latin: "about")
CAB	Citizens Advice Bureau (British)
CAB	Civil Aeronautics Board (defunct U.S. agency; see FAA below)
cabal	Clifford, Arlington, Buckingham, Ashley, Lauderdale (ministers of Charles II of England; one explanation of derivation of "cabal")
CAN	Canada
CAO	Carolina Freight Corporation
cap.	Capital
CAP	Civil Air Patrol (U.S.)
CARE	Cooperative for American Relief Everywhere
CAT	Computerized axial tomography (usually seen as CATscan)
CATscan	CAT (see above) scanner
CATV	Cable television
CATV	Community antenna television
CB	Citizens' band (radio)
CB	Companion of the Bath (British honor)
CB	Seabee; U.S. Navy *c*onstruction *b*attalion

CBA	Canadian Bankers Association
CBA	Canadian Booksellers Association
CBA	Christian Broadcasting Association
CBC	Canadian Broadcasting Corporation
CBC	Complete blood count
CBD	Central business district
CBE	Commander of the Order of the British Empire
CBI	China-Burma-India, World War II theater of operations
CBI	Confederation of British Industry
CBI	*Cumulative Book Index* (publication)
CBM	Continental ballistic missile
CBN	Christian Broadcasting Network
CBO	Congressional Budget Office
CBOE	Chicago Board Options Exchange
CBOT	Chicago Board of Trade
CBS	Columbia Broadcasting System (radio and television network)
CBT	Chicago Board of Trade
CC	Canadian Club whiskey

cc	Carbon copy
CC	Carson City (mint mark on U.S. coins)
cc	Cubic centimeter (.000001 cubic meter)
CCC	Civilian Conservation Corps (New Deal agency providing employment for young men in reclamation and building projects; defunct)
CCCP	Russian for USSR (see below)
CCH	Commerce Clearing House (publisher)
CCU	Coronary care unit (in a hospital)
Cd	Cadmium (element)
cd	Candle (unit of illumination)
CD	Certificate of deposit
CD	Civil Defense (U.S.)
CD	Compact disk
CDC	Centers for Disease Control (U.S. agency for research on communicable diseases)
CDT	Central Daylight Time
Ce	Cerium (element)
CE	Chemical or civil engineer
CE	Continuing education

CEA	Council of Economic Advisors (U.S. presidential advisory group on fiscal policy)
CEGB	Central Electricity Generating Board (of Great Britain)
cent.	Century
CENTO	Central Treaty Organization (defunct; mutual assistance and defense treaty in Central Asia)
CEO	Chief executive officer
CETA	Comprehensive Employment and Training Act (U.S. jobs program 1973-1982)
Cf	Californium (element)
cf.	Confer (Latin: "compare")
CF	Consolidated Foods
CF	Consolidated Freightways, Inc.
CFL	Canadian Football League
CFO	Chief financial officer
CFTC	Commodity Futures Trading Commission (U.S. agency regulating futures markets)
cg	Centigram (.01 gram)
CG	Columbia Gas System, Inc.
ch.	Chapter

CH	Companion of Honour (British honor)
chap.	Chapter
chem.	Chemical
CHiPs	California Highway Patrol (used for TV series)
chm.	Chairman
chmn.	Chairman
Chr.	Chronicles (book of the Bible)
CHUNNEL	(English) Channel tunnel
CHV	Chevron Corporation
CI	Channel Islands
CIA	Central Intelligence Agency (U.S. agency for foreign intelligence operations; see also OSS below)
CIC	Commander in Chief (usually refers to U.S. president; see also C-in-C below)
CID	Criminal Investigation Dept. (generic, but generally refers to Scotland Yard)
CIM	Computer integrated manufacturing
C-in-C	Commander in Chief
CIO	Congress of Industrial Organizations (coalition of industrial unions; see also AFL-CIO above)

CIP	Cataloging-in-Publication
Cl	Chlorine (element)
CLE	Cleveland, Ohio airport
CLI	Cost of living index
CLT	Charlotte, North Carolina airport
cm	Centimeter (.01 meter)
Cm	Curium (element)
cm^2	Square centimeter (.0001 square meter)
cm^3	Cubic centimeter (.000001 cubic meter)
CME	Chicago Mercantile Exchange
CMH	Columbus, Ohio airport
CMO	Chief Medical Officer (U.S. military)
CN	Canada
cn	Night/off peak business coach (airfare)
CNA	Continental National America (insurance company)
CND	Campaign for Nuclear Disarmament (Great Britain)
CNF	Consolidated Freightways, Inc.
CNG	Consolidated Natural Gas Company

CNN	Cable News Network
C-note	U.S. $100 bill
CNP	Canadian Northern Pacific Railway
CNR	Canadian National Railways
CNW	Chicago and Northwestern Transportation Company
CO	Carbon monoxide
c/o	Care of
Co	Cobalt (element)
CO	Colorado (U.S. postal code)
CO	Commanding officer (U.S. military)
CO	Conscientious objector (to service in the armed forces)
CO	Continental Airlines
C & O	Chesapeake & Ohio Railway (now CSX; see below)
CO$_2$	Carbon dioxide
COBOL	Common Business-Oriented Language (computer language)
COC	Chamber of Commerce (generic for business organizations at local, state, and national level; see also C of C below)

coch	Spoonful (prescription note)
cochl	Spoonfuls (prescription note)
COD	Cash on delivery
coed	Coeducational or woman college student
C of C	Chamber of Commerce (see COC above)
C of E	Church of England
C of L	Cost of living
COI	Central Office of Information (Great Britain)
Col.	Colonel
Col.	Colossians (book of the Bible)
col.	Column
COLA	Cost of living adjustment or allowance
COM	Computer output microfilm or microform
comb.	Combining/combination
COMECON	Council for Mutual Economic Assistance (trade/economic group of Soviet-bloc countries)
COMEX	Formerly New York Commodities Exchange
Comintern	Communist International

comm.	Committee
comm.	Community/committee
comp.	Compilation
comp.	Compiler
comp.	Composer
compar.	Comparative
COMSAT	Communications Satellite Corporation
CONELRAD	Control of electromagnetic radiations (U.S. defense mechanism)
conj.	Conjunction
Conrail	Consolidated Rail Corporation
constr.	Construction
cont.	Continued
contr.	Contraction
COO	Chief operating officer
Cor.	Corinthians (book of the Bible)
CORE	Congress of Racial Equality (civil rights group)
Corp.	Corporation
CP	Canadian Pacific Limited

CP	Communist Party
CPA	Certified public accountant
CPA	Communist Party of America
CPB	Corporation for Public Broadcasting (U.S. agency providing some funds for PBS and NPR [see below] stations)
CPI	Consumer Price Index
CPO	Chief Petty Officer (U.S. or British Navy)
CPR	Cardiopulmonary resuscitation (first-aid technique)
CPU	Central processing unit (of a computer)
Cr	Chromium (element)
CREF	College Retirement Equities Fund (pension fund)
CRT	Cathode ray terminal or tube
Cs	Cesium (element)
CSA	Confederate States of America
CSO	Chicago Symphony Orchestra
CSS	Confederate States Ship
CST	Central Standard Time

CSX	CSX Corporation (formed by merger of the Chessie System and Seaboard Coast Line Railroad)
CT	Connecticut (U.S. postal code)
CTA	Chicago Transit Authority
CTN	New York Cotton Exchange
Cu	Cuprum (element, copper)
cu cm	Cubic centimeter (.000001 cubic meter)
cu ft	Cubic foot
cu in	Cubic inch
CUNY	City University of New York
CUP	Cambridge University Press
cu yd	Cubic yard
CV	Convertible security
CVG	Cincinnati, Ohio airport
CVX	Cleveland Electric Illuminating Company
CW	Colonial Williamsburg
CWE	Commonwealth Edison Company
CWP	Communist Workers Party
cwt	hundredweight (long or short, 100 or 112 pounds, respectively)

CWU	Chemical Workers' Union
CX	Centerior Energy
CYO	Catholic Youth Organization
CZ	Canal Zone (former U.S. possession in Panama)
CZ	Combat zone

D

D	Business class discounted (airfare)
d.	Deceased
d.	Died
D	December
D	Denver (mint mark on U.S. coins)
D	Dinner (flight)
D	Five hundred (Roman numeral)
3-D	Three-dimensional
DA	District Attorney
DAB	*Dictionary of American Biography* (publication)
dag	Dekagram (10 grams)
DAI	*Dissertations Abstracts International* (publication)

dal	Dekaliter (10 liters)
dam	Dekameter (10 meters)
Dan.	Daniel (book of the Bible)
DAR	Daughters of the American Revolution
dau	Daughter
D & B	Dun and Bradstreet (publisher)
DBE	Dame Commander of the Order of the British Empire
DBF	Divorced black female
DBM	Divorced black male
dc	*Da capo* (Italian: "from the beginning"; musical direction)
DC	Decimal Classification
DC	Direct current
DC	Disciples of Christ (church)
DC	District of Columbia (U.S. postal code)
DC (numeral)	Airplane built by McDonnell Douglas Corporation
D & C	Dilation and curettage (medical procedure)
DCA	Washington, D.C. airport (National Airport)

Dcb.	December
DCM	Distinguished Conduct Medal (British military honor)
DD	Doctor of Divinity
DD	Du Pont (E.I.) de Nemours & Company
DDC	Dewey Decimal Classification
DDD	Direct distance dialing
DDR	Deutsche Demokratische Republik (East Germany)
DDS	Doctor of Dental Science
DDT	Dichlorodiphenyltri-chloroethane (insecticide)
DE	Delaware (U.S. postal code)
DE	Department of Employment (Great Britain)
DEA	Drug Enforcement Administration (U.S. agency)
Dec.	December
def.	Definite
DEN	Denver, Colorado airport
deriv.	Derivative

DET	Detroit, Michigan airport
DFA	Doctor of Fine Arts (academic degree)
DFC	Distinguished Flying Cross (U.S. or British military decoration)
DFW	Dallas/Fort Worth, Texas airport
dg	Decigram (.10 gram)
DGG	Deutsche Grammophon Gesellschaft (German recording company)
DHSS	Department of Health and Social Security (Great Britain)
DI	Drill instructor (U.S. Marines)
dial.	Dialect
dial.	Dialogue
dim.	Diminutive
dist.	District
div.	Division
DIY	Do it yourself
DJ	Dinner jacket
DJ	Disc jockey
DJ	Doctor Juris (academic degree)

DJ	Dow Jones
DJIA	Dow Jones Industrial Average
DJTA	Dow Jones Transportation Average
DJTU	Dow Jones Utility Average
dl	Deciliter (.10 liter)
DL	Delta Air Lines
dm	Decimeter (0.1 meter)
DM	Deutsche Mark (German monetary unit, usually referring to West Germany)
dm³	Cubic decimeter (.001 cubic meter or 1 liter)
DMS	Data management system (computer program)
DMZ	Demilitarized zone
DN	Diploma in Nursing
DNA	Deoxyribonucleic acid
DNB	*Dictionary of National Biography* (British publication)
DOA	Dead on arrival
DoD	U.S. Dept. of Defense
DOE	U.S. Dept. of Education

DOE	U.S. Dept. of Energy
DoE	Department of the Environment (Great Britain)
DOS	Disk Operating System (computer program)
DoT	Department of Trade (Great Britain)
DOT	Dept. of Transportation (generic for a government agency)
DP	Data processing (see also EDP below)
DP	Displaced person (usually applied to a refugee)
DPT	Diptheria and tetanus toxids with pertussis (inoculation)
DR	Dining room
Dr.	Doctor
dr	dram (.0625 ounce)
DRV	Democratic Republic of Vietnam (once only applicable to North Vietnam)
DSB	*Dictionary of Scientific Biography* (publication)
DSC	Distinguished Service Cross (U.S. and British military decoration)
DSc.	Doctor of Science (academic degree)

DSM	Distinguished Service Medal (U.S. and British military decoration)
DSO	Distinguished Service Order (British military decoration)
d.s.p.	*Decessit sine prole* (Latin: "died without issue")
DST	Daylight Savings Time
DT	Daylight time
Dt.	Deuteronomy (book of the Bible)
DTE	Detroit Edison Company
DTH	Dance Theater of Harlem
DTs	*Delirium tremens* (Latin: refers to hallucinations experienced by alcoholics)
DTT	Detroit, Michigan airport
DTW	Detroit, Michigan airport
DV	Douay Version (of the Bible)
DWF	Divorced white female
DWI	Driving while under the influence (of alcohol, usually); driving while intoxicated
DWM	Divorced white male
dwt	Pennyweight (.05 ounce; see also pwt)
Dy	Dysprosium (element)

E

E	East
E	Effective
E	Effort
E	English
E	Excellence
E	Shoe width for a man's size (up to EEEE, the widest)
ea.	Each
EA	Eastern Air Lines, Inc.
EAL	Eastern Air Lines, Inc.
EB	*Encyclopaedia Britannica* (publication)
Ec.	Ecclesiastes (book of the Bible)
Eccles.	Ecclesiastes (book of the Bible)

ECG	Electrocardiogram (see also EKG below)
econ.	Economic
econ.	Economics
econ.	Economist
ECSC	European Coal and Steel Community (part of EEC; see below)
ED	Consolidated Edison Company of New York
ed.	Edited
ed.	Editor
EDC	European Defense Community
edn.	Education
ednl.	Educational
EDP	Electronic data processing (see also DP above, now more common)
EDT	Eastern Daylight Time
EE	Electrical engineer
EE	Shoe width for a man's size
EEC	European Economic Community (usually referred to as the Common Market; customs and trade union of European countries)

EEE	Shoe width for a man's size
EEEE	Shoe width for a man's size (widest size)
EEG	Electroencephalogram
EEO	Equal employment opportunity
EEOC	Equal Employment Opportunity Commission (U.S. agency enforcing nondiscriminatory hiring policies)
EFT	Electronic funds transfer
EFTA	European Free Trade Association (customs union)
e.g.	*Exempli gratia* (Latin: "for example")
EK	Eastman Kodak Company
EKG	Electrocardiogram (see also ECG above)
El	Elevated railway
ElHi	Elementary/high school (term used in textbook publishing to indicate target market)
Emcee	Master of Ceremonies (see also MC below)
EMI	Electric and Musical Industries (recording company; acronym now official name)
EMS	European Monetary System

EMT	Emergency medical technician
enc.	Enclosure
ENE	East-northeast
Eng.	England
Eng.	English
engr.	Engineer
engr.	Engrave(d)
ENT	Ear, nose, and throat
EO	Executive Order (issued by U.S. president)
EP	European Parliament
EPA	Environmental Protection Agency (generic for government agency regulating environmental matters)
EPCOT	Experimental Prototype Community of Tomorrow (usually coupled with "Center" and refers to theme park adjacent to Walt Disney World)
Eph.	Ephesians (book of the Bible)
equiv.	Equivalent
ER	Elizabetha Regina (Latin: Queen Elizabeth)
ER	Emergency room

Er	Erbium (element)
ERA	Earned run average (baseball)
ERA	Equal Rights Amendment
ERIC	Educational Resources (was Research) Information Center (U.S. agency disseminating data on educational research and resources)
ERISA	Employee Retirement Income Security Act
ERS	Economic Research Service (U.S. agency in the U.S. Dept. of Agriculture studying agriculture, farming, and related topics)
ERTA	Economic Recovery Tax Act of 1981
Es	Einsteinium (element)
ESA	European Space Agency (multinational space organization, roughly comparable to NASA; see below)
ESC	Economic and Social Council (of the United Nations)
esc.	Escape
ESE	East-southeast
ESN	Educationally subnormal
ESOP	Employee Stock Ownership Plan
esp.	Especially

ESP	Extrasensory perception
Esq.	Esquire
ESSO	Standard Oil trademark, replaced in U.S. by Exxon
EST	Eastern Standard Time
Est.	Esther (book of the Bible)
est.	Estimate(d)
ET	Extra-terrestial (alien)
ETA	Estimated time of arrival
ETA	Euzkadi ta Azkatasuna (Basque: Basque Nation and Liberty, nationalist/terrorist group)
et al.	*Et alii* (Latin: "and others")
Et cetera	(Latin: "and so forth")
ETD	Estimated time of departure
ETO	European Theater of Operations (World War II)
ETS	Educational Testing Service
et seq.	*Et sequens* (Latin: "and the following")
Eu	Europium (element)
EURAILPASS	European Railway passenger ticket

eV	Electron volt (energy unit used in nuclear physics)
EWR	Newark, New Jersey airport
ex.	Except
Ex.	Exodus (book of the Bible)
exc.	Except
exec.	Executive
EZ	Enterprise Zone
Ez.	Ezekiel (book of the Bible)
Ez.	Ezra (book of the Bible)
Ezek.	Ezekiel (book of the Bible)

F

F	Fahrenheit
F	Failure
F	False
F	February
F	Fiction
F	First Class (airfare)
F	Flunk
F	Fluorine (element)
f	*forte* (Italian: "loud"; musical direction)
F	Franc (monetary unit of France)
F	French
F	Friday

4-F	Draft classification; not eligible
F (Plan)	Fiber Plan (diet)
FA	Football Association (Great Britain)
FAA	Federal Aviation Administration (U.S. agency responsible for civil aviation)
Fannie Mae	See FNMA below
FAO	Food and Agriculture Organization (affiliated with the United Nations)
FASB	Financial Accounting Standards Board (of the American Institute of Certified Public Accountants)
FAX	Facsimile
FAX	Facsimile transmission
Fb.	February
FBI	Federal Bureau of Investigation (U.S. agency for criminal investigations)
FCC	Federal Communications Commission (U.S. agency regulating the broadcasting industry)
FCO	Foreign and Commonwealth Office (Great Britain)
FD	Fire department (generic for a government agency, usually preceded by initials of a locality)

FDA	Food and Drug Administration (U.S. agency overseeing food and pharmaceutical industries)
FDIC	Federal Deposit Insurance Corporation (U.S. agency insuring individual bank accounts; see also FSLIC below)
fdn.	Foundation
FDR	Franklin Delano Roosevelt
FDS	Feminine Deodorant Spray (brand name)
FDX	Federal Express Corp.
Fe	Ferrum (element, iron)
Feb.	February
FEC	Federal Elections Commission (U.S. agency administering federal election laws)
FEDLINK	Federal Library and Information Network
FEIN	Federal Employer Identification Number (numeric identifier for tax reporting and other purposes)
fem.	Feminine
FERMILAB	Fermi National Accelerator Laboratory Batavia, Illinois (physics research facility)
ff	Following page(s)
ff	*Fortissimo* (Italian: "very loud"; musical direction)

FFA	Future Farmers of America
fff	*Fortississimo* (Italian: "as loud as possible"; musical direction)
FHA	Federal Highway Administration (U.S. agency administering federal road programs)
FHA	Federal Housing Administration (U.S. agency overseeing federal housing policy)
FHA	Future Homemakers of America
FHLMC	Federal Home Loan Mortgage Corporation ("Freddie Mac")
FICA	Federal Insurance Contributions Act (Social Security contributions as seen on paycheck stubs)
fid. def.	*Fidei defensor* (Latin: "defender of the faith")
fig.	Figure
FL	Florida (U.S. postal code)
Fl	Flourine (element)
fld.	Field
fl dr	Fluid dram
fl oz	Fluid ounce
Fm	Fermium (element)

FM	Field Marshall (military rank)
FM	Foreign minister or ministry
FM	Frequency modulation (broadcasting system)
Fn	Night/off peak coach in first class compartment (airfare)
FNMA	Federal National Mortgage Association ("Fannie Mae")
FO	Foreign Office (generic for a government agency)
FOB	Free or freight on board
FOE	Fraternal Order of Eagles
FOIA	Freedom of Information Act (U.S. law providing for public disclosure of government documents, etc.)
FOP	Fraternal Order of Police
FORTRAN	Formula translation (computer language)
FP	Fireplace
Fr.	Father (religious address)
FR	Franc (monetary unit of France)
FR	France
Fr	Francium (element)

Fr.	French
Fr.	Friday
FRB	Federal Reserve Bank or Board (U.S. monetary control agency)
Freddie Mac	See FHLMC, above
freq.	Frequency
Fri.	Friday
FSLIC	Federal Savings and Loan Insurance Corporation (U.S. agency insuring individual accounts in savings and loans associations; see also FDIC above)
FSO	Foreign Service Officer in U.S. Dept. of State
ft	Foot
Ft.	Fort
ft²	Square foot (see also sq ft below)
ft³	Cubic foot
FTA	Future Teachers of America
FTC	Federal Trade Commission (U.S. agency enforcing antitrust laws, fair advertising, labeling of products, etc.)
FTD	Florists' Transworld Delivery
FTE	Full-time employee or equivalent

FTI	Financial Times Index
FTZ	Federal or Foreign Trade Zone (duty-free zones on U.S. soil)
FWP	Federal Writers' Project (New Deal program for writers, famous for producing series of travel guides to the states)
FY	Fiscal year

G

G	Gauss (unit of magnetic induction)
G	German
g	Gram
G	Gravity (unit of force)
Ga	Gallium (element)
GA	Gamblers Anonymous
GA	General Assembly (generic for many U.S. state legislatures)
GA	Georgia (U.S. postal code)
GAA	Gay Activists' Alliance
GAAP	Generally Accepted Accounting Principles
Gal.	Galatians (book of the Bible)
gal	Gallon

GAO	General Accounting Office (U.S. Congress' investigative body)
GAR	Grand Army of the Republic (U.S. Civil War veterans' union)
GASP	Group Against Smokers' Pollution
GATT	General Agreement on Tariffs and Trade (group of countries subscribing to mutually agreeable trade policies; affiliated with the United Nations)
GATX	General American Transportation Corporation (acronym now official name)
GAU	Gay Academic Union
GB	Great Britain
GBF	Gay black female
GBAT	Graduate Business Admission Test
GBH	Grievous bodily harm
GBM	Gay black male
GC	George Cross (British military decoration)
GCB	Knight Grand Cross of the Order of the Bath (British honor)
GCHQ	Government Communications Headquarters (Great Britain)
GCSE	General Certificate of Secondary Education (Great Britain)

Gd	Gadolinium (element)
GDP	Gross domestic product (British GNP; see below)
GDR	German Democratic Republic
GE	General Electric Company
Ge	Germanium (element)
Gen.	General
Gen.	Genesis (book of the Bible)
Ger.	German/Germany
Gestapo	Geheime Staats Polizei (German: Secret State Police, NAZI [see below] organization)
GF	General Foods Corporation
GH	General headquarters
GH	General hospital (generic)
GHQ	General headquarters
ghz	Gigahertz (see below, hz)
GI	Gastro-intestinal (usually with "upper" or "lower" in reference to medical test)
GI	General or government issue (generally used to refer to U.S. soldiers as in "GIs")
gi	Gill (4 fluid ounces)

Ginnie Mae	See GNMA below
Gk.	Greek
GLC	Greater London Council
GLF	Gay Liberation Front (one of the first militant homosexual rights' groups of the late 1960s; defunct)
GM	General medicine
GM	General Motors Corporation
GMAT	General Management Admission Test
GMAT	Greenwich Mean Astronomical Time
GMC	General Medical Council (Great Britain)
GMC	General Motors Corporation (used like a brand name for its trucks)
GMN	Greenwich Mean Noon
GMS	General maintenance system (computer program)
GMT	Greenwich Mean Time
GNMA	Government National Mortgage Association ("Ginnie Mae")
GNP	Gross national product
GNS	Gannett News Service
GOC	General Officer Commanding (Great Britain)

GOM	Grand Old Man (originally a nickname for British Prime Minister William Gladstone; now sometimes applied to a distinguished older person in a profession)
GOP	Grand Old Party (Republican Party)
Gov.	Governor
govt.	Government
GP	General practitioner (medicine)
GP	Gray Panthers (senior citizens' group)
GP	Parental Guidance Suggested (rating for movies; now PG, see below)
GPA	Grade point average
GPM	Graduated payment mortgage
GPO	General Post Office (Great Britain)
GPO	Government Printing Office (U.S. agency charged with publishing and printing federal reports, documents, etc.)
GQ	*Gentlemen's Quarterly* (publication)
gr	Grain (.002286 ounce)
grad.	Graduate(d)
GRAS	Generally regarded or recognized as safe (FDA [see above] rating)
Gr. Brit.	Great Britain

GRE	Graduate Record Examination
G & S	Gilbert and Sullivan
GSA	General Services Administration (U.S. agency for property management, procurement, etc.)
GSA	Girl Scouts of America
GSLP	Guaranteed Student Loan Program
GSO	General Staff Officer (Great Britain)
gt	Drop (prescription note)
GT	Goodyear Tire & Rubber Company
GT	Greenwich Time
GTA	Graduate teaching assistant
GTE	General Telephone and Electronics Corporation (acronym now official name)
gtt	Drops (prescription note)
GU	Guam (U.S. postal code)
GVN	Government of Vietnam
G & W	Gulf and Western Industries
GWF	Gay white female
GWM	Gay white male
GWTW	*Gone With the Wind* (publication and movie)

H

H	Coach economy discounted (airfare)
H	Height
h	Hour
H	House (of Representatives; in Congress and U.S. state legislatures)
H	Hydrogen (element)
H	U.S. military designation (when paired with another letter) for a search and rescue aircraft
4-H	Organization for youth, emphasizing "head, heart, hands, and health"
H (bomb)	Hydrogen bomb
HA	Housing authority (generic for a government agency, usually preceded by the applicable initial as in CHA, Chicago Housing Authority)

Hab.	Habakkuk (book of the Bible)
HABS	Historic American Buildings Survey (collection of drawings and photos of historic American structures, housed at the Library of Congress)
Hag.	Haggai (book of the Bible)
HB	Halfback (in football)
HB	Hard black (pencil)
HB	House bill (in Congress and U.S. state legislatures)
HBC	History Book Club (mail order book club)
HBMS	Her/His Britannic Majesty's Service or Ship
HBO	Home Box Office
HC	Hot and cold (water)
HC	House of Commons (British Parliament; see also H of C below)
HCL	High cost of living
HCR	House concurrent resolution (in Congress and U.S. state legislatures)
He	Helium (element)
Heb.	Hebrews (book of the Bible)
HEW	U.S. Dept. of Health, Education, and

Welfare (defunct; replaced by Departments of Education and Health and Human Services)

Hf	Hafnium (element)
HFC	Household Finance Corporation
hg	Hectogram (100 grams)
Hg	Hydrargyrum (element, mercury)
HGV	Heavy goods vehicle (British)
HH	His/Her Highness
HHS	U.S. Dept. of Health and Human Services
HI	Hawaii (U.S. postal code)
HiFi	High fidelity; also a publication
hl	Hectoliter (100 liters)
hm	Hectometer (100 meters)
HM	Her/His Majesty('s)
HMO	Health maintenance organization
HMS	Her/His Majesty's Service or Ship
HMSO	Her/His Majesty's Stationery Office (British government printer)
HNC	Higher National Certificate (Great Britain)
HND	Higher National Diploma (Great Britain)

HNL	Honolulu, Hawaii airport
Ho	Holmium (element)
H of C	House of Commons (British Parliament; see also HC above)
HoJo	Howard Johnson's restaurant
Hon.	Honourable (British title)
Hos.	Hosea (book of the Bible)
HOU	Houston Industries Incorporated
HOU	Houston, Texas airport
HP	Hire purchase (British)
HP	Horsepower
HQ	Headquarters
HR	Holiday route
HR	Home run (baseball)
hr.	Hour
HR	House of Representatives (Congress and U.S. state legislatures)
HR	House report or resolution (in Congress and U.S. state legislatures)
HRE	Holy Roman Empire (defunct)
HRH	Her/His Royal Highness

HS	High school
HS	Hospital ship
HSH	Her/His Serene Highness
HTLV	Human T-cell leukemia and/or lymphotropic virus
HUAC	House Un-American Activities Committee (in Congress)
HUD	U.S. Department of Housing and Urban Development
hz	Hertz (unit of frequency of radio waves, usually seen as kilohertz (khz), megahertz (mhz) or gigahertz (ghz)

I

I	Interstate (highway when coupled with a number)
I	Iodine (element)
I	Island(s)
I	One (Roman numeral)
IA	Iowa (U.S. postal code)
IAD	Washington, D.C. airport (Dulles)
IAEA	International Atomic Energy Agency (affiliated with the United Nations)
IAH	Houston, Texas airport
ibid.	*Ibidem* (Latin: "in the same place")
IBM	Intercontinental ballistic missile
IBM	International Business Machines Corporation

IBRD	International Bank for Reconstruction and Development (affiliated with the United Nations)
IC	Intensive care (hospital ward)
ICA	Institute of Contemporary Arts (Great Britain)
ICAO	International Civil Aviation Organization (affiliated with the United Nations)
ICBM	Intercontinental ballistic missile
ICC	Interstate Commerce Commission (U.S. agency regulating interstate transportation companies)
ICI	Imperial Chemical Industries Company
ICJ	International Court of Justice (affiliated with the United Nations)
ICMA	International City Management Association
ICU	Intensive care unit (in a hospital)
ID	Idaho (U.S. postal code)
id.	*Idem* (Latin: "same")
ID	Identification
IDA	International Development Association (affiliated with the United Nations)
i.e.	*Id est* (Latin: "that is")

IESS	*International Encyclopedia of the Social Sciences* (publication)
IFAA	International Flight Attendants Association (union)
IFAD	International Fund for Agricultural Development (affiliated with the United Nations)
IFC	International Finance Corporation (affiliated with the United Nations)
IGA	Independent Grocers Alliance Distributing Company
IGY	International Geophysical Year
IH	International Harvester Company (now Navistar)
IHOP	International House of Pancakes (restaurant chain)
IHS	*In hoc signo (vinces)* (Latin: "in this sign [you will conquer]"; phrase supposedly revealed to the Roman Emperor Constantine before a battle, along with the Christian cross; popularly, "In His Sign")
II	Two (Roman numeral)
III	Three (Roman numeral)
IL	Illinois (U.S. postal code)
ILA	International Longshoremen's Association (union)

ILGWU	International Ladies' Garment Workers' Union
ILLINET	Illinois Library and Information Network
ILO	International Labor Organization (affiliated with the United Nations)
IMAW (U)	International Molders' and Allied Workers' (union)
IMCO	International Maritime Consultative Organization (affiliated with the United Nations)
IMF	International Monetary Fund (affiliated with the United Nations)
IMM	International Money Market (at the Chicago Mercantile Exchange)
imper.	Imperative
IMS	Information management system (computer program)
in	Inch
IN	Indiana (U.S. postal code)
In	Indium (element)
in²	Square inch
in³	Cubic inch
Inc.	Incorporated

ind.	Independent
IND	Indianapolis, Indiana airport
indef.	Indefinite
indic.	Indicative
INLA	Irish National Liberation Army
INN	Independent News Network
INRI	*Iesus Nazarenus Rex Iudaeorum* (Latin: "Jesus of Nazareth, King of the Jews"; posted at the crucifixion of Jesus by the Romans)
INS	Immigration and Naturalization Service (U.S. agency)
ins.	Insurance
inst.	Institute
inst.	Institution
INTELSAT	International Telecommunications Satellite (trademark)
intercom	Intercommunications system
interj.	Interjection
Interpol	International Police Organization
IOC	International Olympic Committee
IOU	I owe you

IP	International Paper Company
IPA	International Police Association
IQ	Intelligence quotient (result of a psychological/educational test)
Ir	Iridium (element)
Ir.	Irish
IRA	Individual retirement account
IRA	Irish Republican Army (nationalist/terrorist group)
IRBM	Intermediate range ballistic missile
IRC	Internal Revenue Code (U.S. income tax laws)
IRC	International Red Cross
Ire.	Ireland
irreg.	Irregular
IRS	Internal Revenue Service (agency in the U.S. Dept. of the Treasury)
Is.	Isaiah (book of the Bible)
ISBN	International Standard Book Number (unique identifier for each published book)
ISO	International Standards Organization; International Organization for Standardiza-

tion (now used for film speed designations, replacing ASA [see above] on film rolls)

ISSN	International Standard Serial Number (unique identifier for each periodical title)
It.	Italian
It.	Italy
ital.	Italic (type)
ITC	Investment tax credit (against U.S. income tax liability)
ITT	International Telephone and Telegraph Corporation
ITU	International Telecommunication Union (affiliated with the United Nations)
ITV	Independent Television (Great Britain)
IUCD	Intrauterine contraceptive device
IUD	Intrauterine device
IV	Four (Roman numeral)
IV	Intravenous
IVF	In vitro fertilization (of embryos)
IWW	Industrial Workers of the World ("Wobblies"; radical labor organization espousing syndicalism)
IX	Nine (Roman numeral)

J

J	Business class premium (airfare)
J	January
j	Joule (unit of work)
J	July
J	June
Ja.	January
JA	Junior Achievement
JAL	Japan Air Lines
Jan.	January
JAP	Jewish-American prince or princess (in some contexts, may be considered derogatory)
Jas.	James (book of the Bible)

JAYCEES	Junior Chamber of Commerce (acronym now official name; see also JCC below)
JC	Jesus Christ
JCC	Junior Chamber of Commerce (see JAYCEES above)
JCI	JAYCEES International
JCS	Joint Chiefs of Staff (of the U.S. military)
JD	Juris/Jurum Doctor (Latin: Doctor of Jurisprudence/Laws; academic degree)
JD	Juvenile delinquent
JDL	Jewish Defense League (group prepared to use violence to defend and protect Jews and Jewish interests)
Je.	June
Jer.	Jeremiah (book of the Bible)
JFK	John Fitzgerald Kennedy
JFK	Kennedy International Airport, New York
Jg.	Judges (book of the Bible)
Jl.	Joel (book of the Bible)
Jl.	July
Jn.	John (book of the Bible)

1 Jn.	1 John (book of the Bible)
2 Jn.	2 John (book of the Bible)
3 Jn.	3 John (book of the Bible)
Jn.	June
Jon.	Jonah (book of the Bible)
Jos.	Joshua (book of the Bible)
Jp.	Japanese
JP	Justice of the Peace
JR	John Ross Ewing, Jr. (of TV series "Dallas")
JRC	Junior Red Cross
Ju.	June

K

K	Carat
K	Kalium (element)
K	Kelvin (temperature measure)
K	Kindergarten
K	Koechel (number assigned to Mozart's musical composition in a catalog compiled by Ludwig Ritter von Koechel)
K	One thousand
K	Potassium (element)
K	Thrift (airfare)
K (cars)	Chrysler Corporation's front-wheel drive cars
KBE	Knight Commander of the British Empire (British honor)
KC	Kansas City

KC	Kansas City Board of Trade
KC	Kennel Club
kc	kilocycle
KC	Knights of Columbus (Catholic fraternal organization; see also K of C below)
kg	kilogram
KG	Knight of the Order of the Garter (British honor)
1 Kg.	1 Kings (book of the Bible)
2 Kg.	2 Kings (book of the Bible)
KGB	Komitet Gossudarstvennoi Bezopasnosti (Russian: "Committee of State Security," Soviet secret police; successor to NKVD, see below)
Kgs.	Kings (books of the Bible)
khz	kilohertz (see hz above)
Ki.	Kings (books of the Bible)
KIA	Killed in action (military designation for battlefield deaths)
KJV	King James' Version of the Bible; also known as the Authorized Version
KKK	Ku Klux Klan
kl	Kiloliter (1000 liters)

KLM	Koninklijke Luchtvaart Maatschappij (Royal Dutch Airlines)
km	Kilometer
km²	Square kilometer (1,000,000 square meters)
kn	Night/off peak thrift discounted (airfare)
KO	Coca-Cola Company
KO	Knock out (in boxing; see also TKO below)
K of C	Knights of Columbus (see KC above)
KP	Kitchen patrol/police (U.S. military)
KP	Knights of Pythias
Kr	Krypton (element)
KS	Kansas (U.S. postal code)
kw	Kilowatt
KY	Kentucky (U.S. postal code)

L

L	Fifty (Roman numeral)
L	Large (clothing size)
L	Latin
L	Length
l	Liter
L	Loss (sports abbreviation)
L	Lunch
L	Thrift discounted (airfare)
L (numerals)	Airplane built by Lockheed Corporation
La.	Lamentations (book of the Bible)
La	Lanthanum (element)
LA	Library Association (Great Britain)
LA	Los Angeles, California

LA	Louisiana (U.S. postal code)
Laetrile	Laevo-mandelonitrile-beta-glucuronic acid (claimed to be an anticancer medicine)
LA-LA land	Los Angeles area
Lam.	Lamentations (book of the Bible)
LANDSAT	Land satellite (produces images of the earth useful for resource exploration, mapping, agriculture, etc.)
LAPD	Los Angeles Police Dept.
l.a.s.	Label as such (with the name of the drug; prescription note)
LAS	Las Vegas, Nevada airport
Laser	Light amplification by stimulated emission of radiation
Lat.	Latin
lat.	Latitude
LAX	Los Angeles, California airport
LB	Linebacker (in football)
lb	Pound
LBJ	Lyndon Baines Johnson
lbw	Leg before wicket (cricket term)
LC	Library of Congress

LCM	Landing craft, mechanized or medium (U.S. Navy)
LCT	Landing craft, tank (U.S. Navy)
LD	Litterarum Doctor (Latin: Doctor of Letters, academic degree)
LDS	Latter-Day Saint(s) (Church of Jesus Christ of; Mormons)
Leg.	Legislature/legislation
LEM	Lunar Excursion Module
Lev.	Leviticus (book of the Bible)
LF	Left front
LF	Linear foot
LG	Literary Guild (mail order book club)
LGA	LaGuardia Airport, New York
LH	Lufthansa German Airlines
LHS	Left hand side
Li	Lithium (element)
Lib.	Liberal (Party; Great Britain)
Lieut.	Lieutenant
LittD	Litterarum Doctor (Latin: Doctor of Literature, Letters, Humanities, etc., usually an honorary academic degree)

LJ	*Library Journal* (publication)
Lk.	Luke (book of the Bible)
LLD	Legum Doctor (Latin: Doctor of Laws, academic degree)
loc. cit.	*Loco citato* (Latin: "in the place cited")
long.	Longitude
LOT	Polish Airlines
LP	Long playing record
LP	Low pressure
LPG	Liquid propane gas
LPN	Licensed practical nurse
Lr	Lawrencium (element; was Lw)
LR	Left rear
L/R	Left/right
LR	Living room
LSAT	Law School Admissions Test
LSD	Landing ship, dock (U.S. Navy)
LSD	Lysergic acid diethylamide
LSD	Pounds, shillings, and pence (obsolete)
LSE	London School of Economic Science

LST	Landing ship, tank (U.S. Navy)
Lt.	Lieutenant
LTC	Leaseway Transportation Corporation
Lt. Col.	Lieutenant Colonel
Lu	Lutetium (element)
LV	Luncheon voucher
LZ	Landing zone
LZ	Loading zone

M

M	Coach economy discounted (airfare)
M	Majesty
M	March
M	Masculine
M	Masochism
M	May
M	Medium (clothing size)
m	Meter
M	Monday
M	Monsieur (French: mister)
M	One thousand (Roman numeral)
M-1, M-2, M-3	Money measures used by the U.S. Federal Reserve Board

m³	Cubic meter
3M	Minnesota Mining and Manufacturing Company
M-16	U.S. Army rifle
MA	Massachusetts (U.S. postal code)
MA	Master of Arts (academic degree)
Ma.	May
mace	Methylchloroform chloroacetophenone (self-defense chemical)
MACV	Military Assistance Command, Vietnam (U.S. military advisory in South Vietnam)
MAD	Mutual assured destruction (by nuclear weapons)
MADD	Mothers Against Drunk Driving
Mal.	Malachi (book of the Bible)
Mar.	March
masc.	Masculine
MASH	Mobile Army Surgical Hospital (also name of film and TV series)
MAT	Master of Arts in Teaching (academic degree)
max.	Maximum

MB	Manitoba (Canadian province; U.S. postal code)
MBA	Master of Business Administration (academic degree)
MBE	Member of the Order of the British Empire (British honor)
MC	Marine Corps (U.S.)
MC	Master of Ceremonies (see also Emcee above)
MC	MasterCard
MC	Military Cross (British decoration)
MCC	Marylebone Cricket Club
MCC	Metropolitan Community Church
MCC	Mission Control Center, Houston (part of NASA; see below)
MCD	McDonald's Corporation
MCI	Kansas City, Missouri airport
MCI	Microwave Communications of America, Inc.
MCO	Orlando, Florida airport
MCP	Male chauvinist pig (often pejorative)
MD	Managing director

MD	Maryland (U.S. postal code)
MD	Medicinae Doctor (Latin: Doctor of Medicine; academic degree)
Md	Mendelevium (element; also sometimes Mv)
MDT	Mountain Daylight Time
MDW	Chicago, Illinois airport (Midway)
ME	Maine (U.S. postal code)
ME	Methodist Episcopal (church)
ME	Middle East
ME	Middle English
med.	Medical
mem.	Member
MEM	Memphis, Tennessee airport
memb.	Member
MEP	Member, European Parliament
Mex.	Mexican
Mex.	Mexico
MEX	Mexico City, Mexico airport
mf	*Mezzo forte* (Italian: "medium loud"; musical direction)

M-F	Monday through Friday
MFA	Master of Fine Arts (academic degree)
Mg	Magnesium (element)
mg	Milligram (.001 gram)
MG	Cars produced by the British company, Morris Garage
MG	Myasthenia gravis (muscular disease)
mgmt.	Management
MGM	Metro-Goldwyn-Mayer (movie studio)
mgr.	Manager
Mgr.	Monsignor
MHG	Middle High German
mhz	Megahertz (see hz above)
MI	Michigan (U.S. postal code)
mi	Mile
MI	Military Intelligence
mi^2	Square mile (see also sq mi below)
MI-5	Secret Service Division (Great Britain)
MI-6	Espionage, Counter Espionage Department (Great Britain)

MIA	Miami, Florida airport
MIA	Missing in action (U.S. military designation for personnel unaccounted for following a battle)
Mic.	Micah (book of the Bible)
MID	Midwest Stock Exchange
MIG	Mikoyan and Gurevich (name for Soviet military aircraft, after the designers' names)
mil.	Military
min.	Minimum
min.	Minute
MIRAS	Mortgage interest relief at source
MIRV	Multiple independent or independently targetable reentry vehicle (missile type; see also MRV below)
Mk.	Mark (book of the Bible)
MKC	Kansas City, Missouri airport
ML	Middle Latin
ML	Midway Airlines
ml	Milliliter (.001 liter)
MLA	Medical Library Association

MLA	Music Library Association
Mlle.	Mademoiselle (French: "miss")
MLS	Master of Library Science (academic degree)
MLS	Multiple listing service
mm	Millimeter (.001 meter)
Mme.	Madame (French: "missus")
MMM	Minnesota Mining and Manufacturing Company
MMR	Measles, mumps, and rubella (inoculation)
Mn	Manganese (element)
MN	Minnesota (U.S. postal code)
mn.	Month
MO	Medical Officer (U.S. military)
MO	Missouri (U.S. postal code)
MO	*Modus operandi* (Latin: "method of procedure")
Mo	Molybdenum (element)
Mo.	Monday
MO	Money order
mo.	Month

MO	Philip Morris Companies Inc.
MoD	Ministry of Defense (Great Britain)
MOMA	Museum of Modern Art (New York, New York)
Mon.	Monday
mon.	Month
moped	Motor/pedal (motorized bike)
MoT	Ministry of Transport (Great Britain)
motel	Motor hotel (now used as a distinctive word)
MP	Member of Parliament (Great Britain)
MP	Methodist Protestant
MP	Metropolitan police
mp	*Mezzo piano* (Italian: "medium soft," musical direction)
MP	Military Police (U.S. Army)
MP	Mounted police
MPAA	Motion Picture Association of America (movie-rating group)
mpg.	Miles per gallon
MPH	Miles per hour

Mr.	March
MR	Millirem
mr.	Milliroentgen
Mr.	Mister
MRK	Merck & Co., Inc.
MRV	Multiple reentry vehicle (see also MIRV above)
ms.	Manuscript
MS	Master of Science (academic degree)
MS	Mississippi (U.S. postal code)
MS	Multiple sclerosis (neural disease)
MSA	Metropolitan Statistical Area (Bureau of the Census unit; was SMSA, see below)
MSAT	Minnesota Scholastic Aptitude Test
MSE	Montreal Stock Exchange
MSG	Monosodium glutamate (flavor enhancer)
MSP	Minneapolis-St. Paul, Minnesota airport
mss.	Manuscripts
MST	Mountain Standard Time
MSY	New Orleans, Louisiana airport

Mt.	Matthew (book of the Bible)
MT	Mean tide
MT	Mean time
MT	Montana (U.S. postal code)
Mt.	Mountain/Mount
MTV	Music Television
Mv	Mendelevium (element; usually Md)
MV	Motor vehicle
MX	Experimental missile
MX	Multiplex(er)

N

N	Inco Limited
N	Nitrogen (element)
N	North
n	Note
n	Noun
N	November
N/A	Name and address
Na	Natrium (element, sodium)
NA	North America
N/A	Not applicable
NAACP	National Association for the Advancement of Colored People
NAAFI	Navy, Army, and Air Force Institutes (Great Britain)

NADA	National Automobile Dealers Association
Nah.	Nahum (book of the Bible)
NAL	New American Library (publisher)
NALGO	National and Local Government Officers Association (Great Britain)
NAM	National Association of Manufacturers
napalm	Naphthenic and palmitic acids
NARAL	National Abortion Rights Action League
NASA	National Aeronautics and Space Administration (U.S. agency for space exploration and research)
NASD	National Association of Securities Dealers
NASDAQ	National Association of Securities Dealers Automatic Quotations (OTC [see below] stock price quotes)
NATO	North Atlantic Treaty Organization (military alliance of U.S., Canada, and European allies)
naut.	Nautical
NAV	Navistar
NAZI	Nationalsozialistische Deutsche Arbeiterpartei (German: "National Socialist German Workers' Party"; see also NDAP and NSDAP below)

NB	New Brunswick (Canadian province; U.S. postal code)
Nb	Niobium (element)
n.b.	*Nota bene* (Latin: "note well")
NBA	National Basketball Association
NBA	National Book Awards (defunct; see ABA)
NBC	National Broadcasting Company (radio and television network)
N/C	No charge or cost
NC	North Carolina (U.S. postal code)
NCA	North Central Association of Colleges and Secondary Schools; now NCACS, see below; accreditation agency)
NCAA	National Collegiate Athletic Association
NCACS	National Association of Colleges and Schools (see also NCA above)
NCB	National Coal Board (Great Britain)
NCCC	National Conference of Catholic Charities
NCO	Noncommissioned officer (U.S. military)
NCPAC	National Conservative Political Action Committee
NCR	National Cash Register Company (acronym now official name)

NCR	No Canadian rights
Nd	Neodynium (element)
n.d.	No date (of publication)
ND	North Dakota (U.S. postal code)
NDAP	Nationalsozialistische Deutsche Arbeiterpartei (German: "National Socialist German Workers' Party"; see NAZI above and NSDAP below)
NE	Nebraska (U.S. postal code)
Ne	Neon (element)
NE	New England
NE	Northeast
NEA	National Education Association (teachers' union)
NEA	National Endowment for the Arts (U.S. agency awarding project grants)
NEB	New English Bible
NEDC	National Economic Development Council (Great Britain)
NEH	National Endowment for the Humanities (U.S. agency awarding project grants)
Neh.	Nehemiah (book of the Bible)
NET	National Educational Television

neut.	Neuter
NF	National Front (British right-wing party)
NF	Newfoundland (Canadian province; U.S. postal code)
NFC	National Football Conference (defunct)
NFL	National Football League
NFZ	Nuclear free zone
NGA	National Graphical Association (Great Britain)
NGS	National Geographic Society
NH	New Hampshire (U.S. postal code)
NHL	National Hockey League
NHS	National Health Service (Great Britain)
NHS	National Honor Society
NHSA	National Highway Safety Administration (now NHTSA, see below)
NHTSA	National Highway Traffic Safety Administration (U.S. agency)
NI	National insurance
Ni	Nickel (element)
NICU	Neonatal intensive care unit (in a hospital)

NIH	National Institutes of Health (U.S. agency for medical research)
NJ	New Jersey (U.S. postal code)
NKVD	Narodnyi Kommissariat Vnutrennikh Del (Russian: "People's Commissariat of Internal Affairs," Soviet secret police up to 1946; succeeded by KGB, see above)
NL	National League (baseball teams)
NLF	National Liberation Front (generic, but frequently applied to the Vietnamese nationalist group prior to 1975)
NLRA	National Labor Relations Act (U.S.)
NLRB	National Labor Relations Board (U.S. agency regulating union elections, collective bargaining practices, etc.)
NM	New Mexico (U.S. postal code)
NMK	Niagara Mohawk Power Corporation
NNE	North-northeast
NNW	North-northwest
No	Nobelium (element)
no.	Number
nom.	Nominative
NORC	National Opinion Research Center

Nov.	November
NOW	National Organization for Women
Np	Neptunium (element)
n.p.	No place (of publication)
npl.	Noun plural
NPR	National Public Radio
NPS	National Park Service (U.S. agency)
NRA	National Recovery Act (U.S. law, later declared unconstitutional)
NRA	National Recovery Administration (New Deal agency to promote economic recovery; defunct)
NRA	National Restaurant Association
NRA	National Rifle Association
NRC	Nuclear Regulatory Commission (U.S. agency overseeing nuclear power industry)
NROTC	Naval Reserve Officers' Training Corps (U.S.)
NRPC	National Railroad Passenger Corporation (see Amtrak above)
n.s.	New series

NS	Nova Scotia (Canadian province; U.S. postal code)
NSA	National Security Agency (U.S.)
NSC	National Safety Council
NSC	National Security Council (U.S. presidential advisory group on foreign/military policy)
NSC	Norfolk Southern Corporation
NSDAP	Nationalsozialistische Deutsche Arbeiterpartei (German: "National Socialist German Workers' Party"; see also NAZI and NDAP above)
NSF	National Science Foundation (U.S. agency awarding project grants)
NSPCC	National Society for the Prevention of Cruelty to Children (Great Britain)
NT	New Testament (of the Bible)
NTU	National Taxpayers Union
NUJ	National Union of Journalists (Great Britain)
NUM	National Union of Mineworkers (Great Britain)
Num.	Numbers (book of the Bible)

NUPE	National Union of Public Employees (Great Britain)
NUR	National Union of Railwaymen (Great Britain)
NUS	National Union of Students (Great Britain)
NUT	National Union of Teachers (Great Britain)
NV	Nevada (U.S. postal code)
NVA	North Vietnamese Army
Nvb.	November
NW	Northwest
NW	Northwest Orient Airlines
NWA	NWA, Inc. (Northwest Orient Airlines)
NWPC	National Women's Political Caucus
NWT	Northwest Territories (Canada; U.S. postal code)
NY	New York
NYC	New York City
NYCB	New York City Ballet
NYFE	New York Futures Exchange
NYM	New York Mercantile Exchange

NYPD	New York (City) Police Department
NYPL	New York Public Library
NYSE	New York Stock Exchange
NZ	New Zealand

O

O	New Orleans (mint mark on U.S. coins)
O	October
O	Oxygen (element)
OAG	*Official Airline Guide* (publication)
OAK	Oakland, California airport
OAP	Old age pensioner
OAU	Organization of African Unity (association of independent African states)
OAS	Organization of American States (association of U.S. and Latin American states)
Ob.	Obadiah (book of the Bible)
OBE	Order of the British Empire (British honor)
obj.	Object
obj.	Objective

obs.	Obsolete
OCR	Optical character reader or recognition
OCS	Officer Candidate School (U.S. military)
OCS	Optical character scanner
Oct.	October
OE	Old English
OECD	Organization for Economic Cooperation and Development (trade/economic group of free market countries)
OED	*Oxford English Dictionary* (publication)
OH	Ohio (U.S. postal code)
OHMS	On Her/His Majesty's Service
OI	Owens-Illinois, Inc.
OJ	Orange juice
OK	Okay or all correct (British)
OK	Oklahoma (U.S. postal code)
OL	Old Latin
OM	Order of Merit (British honor)
OMB	Office of Management and Budget (U.S. agency charged with development of overall U.S. budget and using such as a management tool)

ON	Ontario (Canadian province; U.S. postal code)
o.o.p.	Out of print
OP	Operating procedure
OP	Operation plan
OP	Other people's cigarettes, money, etc.
o.p.	Out of print
OPA	Office of Price Administration (U.S. agency of World War II)
OPC	Office of Price Control (U.S. agency of World War II)
op. cit.	*Opere citato* (Latin: "in the work cited")
OPD	Out-patient department (in a hospital)
OPEC	Organization of Petroleum Exporting Countries
OP-ED	Opinion/editorial page, usually in a newspaper or magazine
OPM	Office of Personnel Management (U.S. agency, formerly the U.S. Civil Service Commission)
OR	Operating room (hospital)
OR	Operational research
OR	Oregon (U.S. postal code)

ORD	Chicago, Illinois airport (O'Hare; from old name of Orchard Field)
orig.	Origin/original
ORL	Orlando, Florida airport
ORT	Original running time (for movies)
o.s.	Old series
OS	Operating system
Os	Osmium (element)
OS	Out of stock
OSHA	Occupational Safety and Health Administration (U.S. agency regulating workplace safety)
OSS	Office of Strategic Services (U.S. intelligence agency during World War II, forerunner of the CIA; see above)
OT	Occupational therapy
OT	Old Testament (of the Bible)
Otb.	October
OTB	Off-track betting
OTC	Officers' Training Corps (U.S. military)
OTC	Over the counter (stocks)
OTS	Officers' Training School (U.S. military)

OTT	Over the top (too much)
ou	Ounce
OUP	Oxford University Press
OVT	Overnite Transportation Co.
Oxfam	Oxford Committee for Famine Relief (British group)
oz	ounce

P

P	First class premium (airfare)
p.	Page
p	Pence (monetary unit in Great Britain)
P	Philadelphia (mint mark on U.S. coins)
P	Phosphorus (element)
p	*Piano* (Italian: "soft," musical direction)
P	Protestant
PA	Pan American World Airways
PA	Pennsylvania (U.S. postal code)
PA	Personal assistant
PA	Physician's assistant
Pa	Protactinium (element)
PA	Public Act

PA	Public address (system)
PA	Publishers' Association (Great Britain)
PAC	Political action committee (generic for groups formed by parent interest groups for the purpose of raising and distributing money for political campaigns and candidates)
PAIS	*Public Affairs Information Service* (publication)
par.	Paragraph
part.	Participle
pass.	Passive
PATCO	Professional Air Traffic Controllers Organization (union; dissolved)
PAYE	Pay as you earn (British income tax)
pb	Paperback (book)
Pb	Plumbum (element, lead)
PBS	Public Broadcasting System
PC	*Per centum* (Latin: "by the hundred," percent)
PC	Personal computer
PC	Police-constable (British)
PCB	Polychlorinated biphenyl (carcinogen)

PCG	Pacific Gas and Electric Company
PCP	Phenylcyclohexyl piperidine or phencyclidine (carcinogen)
PCS	Postal Commemorative Society (group for collectors of first day covers and commemorative stamps)
Pd	Palladium (element)
PD	Police department (generic for a government agency, usually preceded by initials of a locality)
PDQ	Pretty damn quick
PDT	Pacific Daylight Time
PDX	Portland, Oregon airport
PE	Philadelphia Electric Company
PE	Philadelphia Stock Exchange
PE	Physical education
PEG	Public Service Electric and Gas Company
PEI	Prince Edward Island (Canadian province; U.S. postal code)
PEL	Panhandle Eastern Corporation
Penn.	Pennsylvania
1 Pet.	1 Peter (book of the Bible)

2 Pet.	2 Peter (book of the Bible)
PFC	Private First Class (U.S. Army)
PG	Parental Guidance Suggested (MPAA [see above] movie rating)
PG	Procter & Gamble Company
P & G	Procter & Gamble Company
PG-13	Parental Guidance Suggested, may not be suitable for those under 13 (MPAA [see above] movie rating)
PGA	Professional Golfers' Association
PGL	Peoples Energy Corporation
pH	*Pouvoir hydrogène* (French: "hydrogen power," literally; measure of acidity or alkalinity)
PhD	Doctor of Philosophy
Phil.	Philippians (book of the Bible)
Philem.	Philemon (book of the Bible)
PHL	Philadelphia, Pennsylvania airport
PHX	Phoenix, Arizona airport
PI	Piedmont Aviation
PI	Private investigator
PIE	Piedmont Aviation, Inc.

PIE	Tampa/St. Petersburg, Florida airport
PIK	Payment in kind (U.S. farm support program)
PIN	Personal identification number (for use at an ATM, see above)
PIT	Pittsburgh, Pennsylvania airport
pk	Peck (8 quarts)
pl	Plural
PL	Programming language (for computers)
PL	Public Law
PL/1	Programming Language, Version 1
PLATO	Programmed Logic for Automatic Teaching Operations (computer program)
PLC	Public limited company (comparable to "Inc.")
PLO	Palestine Liberation Organization
PLR	Public lending right
PM	*Post meridiem* (Latin: "after noon")
PM	*Post mortem* (Latin: "after death"; usually refers to dissection of a corpse to determine cause of death)
PM	Prime Minister

Pm	Promethium (element)
PMI	Private mortgage insurance
PMS	Premenstrual syndrome
PN	Pan Am Corporation
PN	Practical nurse
Po	Polonium (element)
PO	Post office
PO	Postal order
PO	Purchase order
P & O	Peninsular & Oriental Steamship Company
POB	Post office box
POE	Port of entry
pol.	Political/politician
Polisario	[Frente] Popular para la Liberacion de Saguia El Hamra y Rio De Oro (Western Sahara nationalist group)
pop.	Population
posh	Port out, starboard home (supposed origin of the word from most desirable cabin location for an Atlantic sea voyage)
POW	Prisoner of war

pp.	Pages
pp	Past participle
pp	*Pianissimo* (Italian: "very soft," musical direction)
p & p	Postage and packing
ppb	Parts per billion
PPG	Pittsburgh Plate Glass Company (acronym is now official name)
pph	Parts per hundred
ppm	Parts per million
PPO	Preferred provider organization (of a health care plan)
ppp	*Pianississimo* (Italian: "as soft as possible"; musical direction)
PPS	*Post postscriptum* (Latin: "after written after," meaning an afterword to an afterword, usually in a personal letter)
PQ	Parti Québecois (Quebec nationalist political party)
PQ	Quebec (Canadian province, U.S. postal code)
PR	Parental recommendation (usually in reference to movie ratings)
Pr	Praseodymium (element)

Pr.	Proverbs (book of the Bible)
PR	Public relations
PR	Puerto Rico (U.S. postal code)
PRC	People's Republic of China
PRC	Postal Rate Commission (U.S. agency setting U.S. Postal Service charges)
pred.	Predicate
prep.	Preposition
PRG	Provisional Revolutionary Government (generally known in the U.S. as the Vietcong)
p.r.n.	As needed (prescription note)
PRO	Public relations officer
prob.	Probably
PROLOG	Programming in Logic (computer language)
pron.	Pronoun
prov.	Province
PS	*Post scriptum* (Latin: "written after," an addendum to a personal letter)
PS	Power steering
Ps.	Psalms (book of the Bible)

PSA	Pacific Southwest Airlines (acronym now official name)
PSAT	Preliminary Scholastic Aptitude Test
PSBR	Public Sector Borrowing Requirement (Great Britain)
PSC	Public Service Commission (generic for government agency regulating public utility companies)
PSE	Pacific Stock Exchange
pseud.	Pseudonym
psi	Pounds per square inch
PST	Pacific Standard Time
pt.	Part
PT	Patrol torpedo boat (Navy designation, usually followed by a number)
Pt.	Peter (book of the Bible)
PT	Physical training
pt	Pint
Pt	Platinum (element)
pt.	Point
PTA	Parent-Teacher Association
PTL	People That Love or Praise the Lord (from TV show "PTL Club")

pto	Please turn over
Pu	Plutonium (element)
pub	Public house (tavern in Great Britain)
pub.	Publication
publ.	Publisher
publ.	Publishing
pubs.	Publications
PUSH	People United to Save Humanity (used as Operation PUSH; civil rights group)
PWA	Public Works Administration (New Deal agency)
pwt	Pennyweight (.05 ounce; see also cwt above)
PX	Post exchange (U.S. military base stores)

Q   Coach economy discounted (airfare)

q.2.h.   Every two hours (prescription note; number can vary)

QANTAS   Queensland and Northern Territory Aerial Service (Australian airline; acronym now official name)

QB   Quarterback (in football)

QC   Queen's counsel (British lawyer)

q.d.   Every day (prescription note)

QE2   Queen Elizabeth 2 (ocean liner)

q.e.d.   *Quod erat demonstrandum* (Latin: "that which was to be shown [or proven]")

q.i.d.   Four times a day (prescription note)

Qn   Night/off peak coach economy (airfare)

QPBC	Quality Paperback Book Club (mail order book club)
Q & Q	*Quill and Quire* (publication)
qt	Quart
quasar	Quasi-stellar
q.v.	*Quod vide* (Latin: "which see"; freely, on the lookout)

R

R	*Regina*/*rex* (Latin: "queen"/"king")
R	Restricted, those under 18 must be accompanied by an adult (MPAA [see above] movie rating)
R	Supersonic (airfare)
3Rs	Reading, (w)riting, and (a)rithmetic
Ra	Radium (element)
RAC	Royal Automobile Association (Great Britain)
RAD	Radiation absorbed dose
RADA	Royal Academy of Dramatic Art (Great Britain)
radar	Radio detection/detecting and ranging
RAF	Royal Air Force (Great Britain)

RAI	Radiotelevisione Italiana (Italian broadcasting company)
RAM	Random access memory
Rb	Rubidium
R & B	Rhythm and blues (musical genre)
RBI	Runs batted in (baseball)
RC	Republic of China
RC	Roman Catholic
RC	Royal Crown (cola)
RCA	Radio Corporation of America (acronym now official name)
RCMP	Royal Canadian Mounted Police
RD	Registered dietician
rd	Rod (16.5 feet)
RD	Rural Delivery (U.S. mail)
R & D	Research and development
rd^2	Square rod (.00625 acre)
RDA	Recommended daily allowance (usually, of vitamins)
RDR	Ryder System, Inc.
RDU	Raleigh/Durham, North Carolina airport

Re	Rhenium (element)
REA	Rural Electrification Administration (U.S. agency)
ref.	Reference
refl.	Reflexive
REIT	Real estate investment trust
rel.	Relative
REM	Rapid eye movement (characteristic of a stage of sleep)
R et I	*Regina/Rex et Imperatrix/Imperator* (Latin: "queen"/"king" and "empress"/"emperor")
Rev.	Revelation (book of the Bible)
rev.	Revolution
RFD	Rural Free Delivery (U.S. mail)
RFP	Request for proposal
RH	Relative humidity
Rh	Rhodium (element)
RHS	Right hand side
RI	Rhode Island (U.S. postal code)
RIBA	Royal Institute of British Architects

RIC	Richmond, Virginia airport
RIF	Reading Is Fundamental (literacy organization)
RIP	*Requiescat in pacem* (Latin: "rest in peace")
RKO	Radio-Keith-Orpheum (movie/broadcasting company)
RLG	Research Libraries Group
RLIN	Research Libraries Information Network
Rn	Radon (element)
RN	Registered nurse
RN	Royal Navy (Great Britain)
RNA	Ribonucleic acid
RNIB	Royal National Institute for the Blind (Great Britain)
R of C	Republic of China
ROK	Republic of Korea
ROM	Read only memory
Rom.	Romans (book of the Bible)
ROTC	Reserve Officers Training Corps (U.S. military)
RPI	Retail Price Index (Great Britain)

RPM	Revolutions per minute
RR	Railroad
RR	Rolls-Royce
RR	Rural route (U.S. mail)
R & R	Rest and relaxation; rest and recuperation; rest and rehabilitation; rest and recovery (U.S. military term for vacations from combat; now used generally for any vacation)
R & R	Rock and roll (musical genre)
R & R	Rock and rye (liquor)
RRSP	Registered Retirement Savings Plan (Canada)
RSC	Royal Shakespeare Company
RSPB	Royal Society for the Protection of Birds (Great Britain)
RSPCA	Royal Society for the Prevention of Cruelty to Animals (Great Britain)
RSR	*Reference Services Review* (publication)
RSV	Revised Standard Version of the Bible
Rsvp	*Répondez s'il vous plaît* (French: "please respond"; request appearing on formal invitations)
RT	Registered trademark

rt.	Route
RT	Running time (for movies)
rte.	Route
Rt. Hon.	(The) Right Honourable (British title)
RTM	Registered trademark
Ru.	Ruth (book of the Bible)
Ru	Ruthenium (element)
RUC	Royal Ulster Constabulary (national police force of Northern Ireland)
RV	Recreational vehicle
Rx	*Recipe* (Latin: "take"; used as shorthand for a medical prescription)

S

S	Sadism/sadist
S	San Francisco (mint mark on U.S. coins)
S	Saturday
S	Schmieder (refers to cataloger of J.S. Bach's musical works, Wolfgang Schmieder, when coupled with a number)
S	Sears, Roebuck & Company
S	Senate (in Congress and U.S. state legislatures)
S	September
S	Small (clothing size)
S	Snack
S	Soprano
S	South

S	Standard class (airfare)
S	Stereo
S	Sulfur (element)
S	Sunday
2-S	Draft classification; student deferral
Sa.	Saturday
sa	See also
SA	Soprano, alto
SA	South America
SA	South Australia
SAA	Soprano, alto (vocal arrangement)
SAA	South African Airlines
SAAB	Name for cars produced by Svenska Aeroplan Aktiebolaget (Swedish company)
SAB	School of American Ballet (New York, New York)
SAB	Soprano, alto, bass (vocal arrangement)
SABENA	Société Anonyme Belge d'Exploitation de la Navigation Aérienne (Belgian airline)
SAC	Strategic Air Command (U.S. Air Force)

SAG	Screen Actors Guild
SALT	Strategic Arms Limitation Talks/Treaty
SAM	Surface to air missile
1 Sam.	1 Samuel (book of the Bible)
2 Sam.	2 Samuel (book of the Bible)
SAN	San Diego, California airport
SANE	National Committee for a Sane Nuclear Policy
SAR	Sons of the American Revolution
SAS	Scandinavian Airlines System
SAS	Special Air Service (British military unit)
SASE	Self-addressed stamped envelope
Sat.	Saturday
SAT	Scholastic Aptitude Test
SATB	Soprano, alto, tenor, bass (vocal arrangement)
SB	Senate bill (in Congress and U.S. state legislatures)
Sb	Stibium (element)
SBA	Small Business Administration (U.S. agency promoting and assisting small businesses)

SBF	Single black female
SBM	Single black male
SBN	Standard Book Number (now ISBN, see above)
SBS	Special Boat Service (British military unit)
Sc	Scandium (element)
sc.	Scene
SC	South Carolina (U.S. postal code)
SCE	Southern California Edison Company
SCI	*Science Citation Index* (publication)
sci-fi	Science fiction
SCLC	Southern Christian Leadership Conference (civil rights group)
SCM	Smith-Corona Marchant (acronym now official name)
SCR	Senate concurrent resolution (in Congress and U.S. state legislatures)
SCTV	"Second City Television" (TV series; name became acronym)
scuba	Self-contained underwater breathing apparatus
SD	South Dakota (U.S. postal code)

SDI	Selective/selected dissemination of information
SDI	Strategic Defense Initiative ("Star Wars")
SDP	Social Democratic Party (Great Britain)
SDS	Students for a Democratic Society
Se	Selenium (element)
SE	Southeast
SEA	Seattle/Tacoma, Washington airport
Seabee	Construction battalion of U.S. Navy (see also CB above)
sec.	Second
sec.	Section
SEC	Securities and Exchange Commission (U.S. agency regulating financial and securities markets)
sec'y	Secretary
sent.	Sentence
Sept.	September
serv.	Service
SF	San Francisco, California
SF	Science fiction

SF	Square foot
SFO	San Francisco, California airport
SFX	Santa Fe Southern Pacific Corp.
S & H	Sperry and Hutchinson Company
SHAEF	Supreme Headquarters, Allied Expeditionary Force (World War II term for Allies' high command in Europe)
SHAPE	Supreme Headquarters, Allied Powers Europe (NATO [see above] headquarters in Europe)
Si	Jet America Airlines
Si	Silicon (element)
SIC	Standard Industrial Classification (numerical scheme or code identifying businesses, used for organizing information around type and kind of business activity)
SID	Sudden infant death syndrome
Simca	Name for cars produced by French company Société Industrielle de Mécanique et de Carrosserie Automobile
sing.	Singular
sitcom	Situation comedy (TV genre)
SJ	Society of Jesus (Roman Catholic order)
SJF	Single Jewish female

SJM	Single Jewish male
SJU	San Juan, Puerto Rico airport
SK	Saskatchewan (Canadian province, U.S. postal code)
S & L	Savings and loan (association)
s.l.	*Sine loco* (Latin: "without place"; generally refers to publications without a named place of publication)
SLA	Special Libraries Association
SLA	Symbionese Liberation Army (Patty Hearst kidnappers)
SLC	Salt Lake City, Utah airport
SLJ	*School Library Journal* (publication)
S & M	Sadism and masochism (sexual practices)
Sm	Samarium (element)
Sm.	Samuel (book of the Bible)
smog	Smoke and fog
SMSA	Standard Metropolitan Statistical Area (unit used by Bureau of the Census; superseded by MSA [see above])
s.n.	*Sine nomine* (Latin: "without name"; generally refers to publications without a named publisher)

Sn	Stannum (element, tin)
S/N	Stock number (when combined with numerals, used as order number for U.S. government publications from GPO [see above])
SNCC	Student Nonviolent (now National) Coordinating Committee (civil rights group)
SNP	Scottish National Party
SOB	Senate Office Building (in Washington, D.C.)
SOB	Son of a bitch (often pejorative)
S of S	Secretary of State
S of S	Song of Songs (book of the Bible; see also SoS below)
Sohio	Standard Oil Company of Ohio
SoHo	South of Houston Street (area of New York City)
SOLINET	Southeastern Library Network
sonar	Sound navigation ranging
SOS	International distress signal in Morse code (supposedly for "save our ship" or "save our souls")
SoS	Song of Songs (book of the Bible; see also S of S above)

SP	Shore Patrol (U.S. Navy police)
S & P	Standard and Poor's Corporation
SPCA	Society for the Prevention of Cruelty to Animals
spp.	Species
SPSS	Statistical Package for the Social Sciences (computer program)
Spt.	September
sq ft	Square foot
sq in	Square inch
sq km	Square kilometer (1,000,000 square meters)
sq mi	Square mile
sq rd	Square rod (.00625 acre)
sq yd	Square yard
SR	Senate report or resolution (in Congress and U.S. state legislatures)
Sr	Señor (Spanish: "mister")
Sr	Strontium (element)
Sra	Señora (Spanish: "missus")
SRA	Supplemental Retirement Annuity

SRN	State registered nurse (Great Britain)
SRO	Single-room occupancy (housing)
SRO	Standing room only
Srta	Señorita (Spanish: "miss")
SS	Secret Service (U.S. security service for high officials)
SS	Steamship
SS	Stosstrupp (German: "shock troop"; NAZI [see above] paramilitary group)
S & S	Simon and Schuster (publisher)
SSA	First soprano, second soprano, alto (vocal arrangement)
SSA	Social Security Administration (U.S. agency handling pension benefits)
SSAA	First soprano, second soprano, first alto, second alto (vocal arrangement)
SSCI	*Social Sciences Citation Index* (publication)
SSE	South-southeast
SSR	Soviet Socialist Republic (component parts of the USSR, see below)
SSS	Selective Service System (U.S. military draft)
SST	Supersonic transport (airplane)

SSW	South-southwest
St.	Saint (male)
ST	Standard Time (generally preceded by initial of a U.S. time zone)
St.	Street
Sta.	Station
STB	Soprano, tenor, bass (vocal arrangement)
STD	Sexually transmitted disease
STD	Subscriber trunk dialing (British version of long distance direct dialing)
Ste.	Saint (female)
Sten	Sheppard, Turpin, England (British submachine gun, using names of inventors)
STL	St. Louis, Missouri airport
STP	Scientifically Treated Petroleum (brand name of motor oil)
Stuka	Sturzkampfflugzeug (German dive bomber in World War II)
Su.	Sunday
subj.	Subject
subj.	Subjunctive

Sun.	Sunday
superl.	Superlative
supp.	Supplement
supr.	Supervisor
supt.	Superintendent
s.v.	*sub verbo* or *voce; sotto voce* (Latin: "under the word," "under the voice," respectively; the latter usually a musical direction meaning very softly)
SVP	Senior vice-president
SW	Southwest
SWAPO	South West Africa People's Organization (Namibian nationalist group)
SWAT	Special weapons and tactics (police units, generally; used with "team")
SWF	Single white female
SWM	Single white male
syn.	Synonym

T	American Telephone & Telegraph Company
T	Coach economy discounted (airfare)
t	Metric ton (1,000,000 grams)
T	Tablespoon
t	Teaspoon
T	Tenor
T	True
Ta	Tantalum (element)
TA	Teaching assistant
TA	Territorial Army (Great Britain)
TABA	The American Book Awards (now ABA, see above)
TB	Tenor, bass (vocal arrangement)

Tb	Terbium (element)
TB	Tuberculosis
TBA	To be announced
TBB	Tenor, baritone, bass (vocal arrangement)
T-bills	Treasury bills (U.S. government securities)
tbsp.	Tablespoon
Tc	Technetium (element)
TC	Telecommunications
TD	Touchdown (in football)
Te	Tellurium (element)
TEFRA	Tax Equity and Fiscal Responsibility Act
TELCOM	Telecommunications
TELECOM	Telecommunications
TES	*Times Educational Supplement* (publication)
TESL	Teaching English as a second language
TexMex	Texas-Mexico (term applied to food, customs, etc. originating in one area and altered by importation into the other)
TF	Task force (generic)

T/F	True/False
TGIF	Thank God it's Friday
Th	Thorium (element)
Th.	Thursday
1 Th.	1 Thessalonians (book of the Bible)
2 Th.	2 Thessalonians (book of the Bible)
THC	Delta-9-tetrahydrocannabinol (active ingredient in marijuana plant)
THES	*Times Higher Educational Supplement* (publication)
Thurs.	Thursday
Ti	Titanium (element)
TIAA	Teachers Insurance and Annuity Association (pension fund)
t.i.d.	Three times a day (prescription note)
1 Tim.	1 Timothy (book of the Bible)
2 Tim.	2 Timothy (book of the Bible)
Tit.	Titus (book of the Bible)
TKO	Technical knock-out (in boxing; see also KO above)
Tl	Thallium (element)

TLA	Theater Library Association
TLC	Tender loving care
TLS	*Times Literary Supplement* (publication)
Tm	Thulium (element)
Tm.	Timothy (book of the Bible)
TM	Trademark
TM	Transcendental meditation
TN	Tennessee (U.S. postal code)
TNT	Trinitrotoluene (explosive)
TNW	Transway International Corporation
TP	Teleprocessing
TP	Title page
TPA	Tampa/St. Petersburg, Florida airport
TR	Theodore Roosevelt
trans.	Translator/translated by
TS	Transsexual
TSE	Toronto Stock Exchange
TSO	Toronto Symphony Orchestra
tsp	Teaspoon

TSS	Toxic shock syndrome
TTB	First tenor, second tenor, bass (vocal arrangement)
TTBB	First tenor, second tenor, baritone, bass (vocal arrangement)
Tu.	Tuesday
TUC	Trades Union Congress (Great Britain)
Tues.	Tuesday
TV	Television
TV	Transvestite
TVA	Tennessee Valley Authority (U.S. electric power and reclamation agency)
TWA	Trans World Airlines
TWU	Transit Workers' Union (of America)
TX	Texaco Inc.
TX	Texas (U.S. postal code)

U

U	No reservation service (airfare)
U	University
U	Uranium (element)
U	USAir Group, Inc.
U-2	U.S. spy airplane
UA	United Air Lines
UAL	United Air Lines
UAR	United Arab Republic (union of Syria and Egypt; defunct)
UAW	United Auto Workers (union)
UBC	Universal bibliographic control
UCC	Uniform Commercial Code
UCC	Uniform Credit Code

UCC	United Church of Christ
UCC	Universal Copyright Convention
UDC	Universal Decimal Classification
UEFA	Union of European Football Associations
UFCW	United Food and Commercial Workers (union)
UFO	Unidentified flying object
UFW	United Farm Workers (union; made famous for its boycotts of lettuce and white grapes)
UHF	Ultrahigh frequency
UHT	Ultra-heat tested (milk testing)
UK	Union Carbide Corporation
UK	United Kingdom (Great Britain)
UL	Underwriters Laboratories (product testing organization)
UMC	United Methodist Church
UMI	University Microfilms International
UMW	United Mine Workers (of America; union)
UN	Union Pacific Corporation
UN	United Nations

UNCTAD	United Nations Conference on Trade and Development
UNDEX	*United Nations Index* (publication)
UNESCO	United Nations Educational, Scientific, and Cultural Organization
UNHCR	United Nations High Commissioner for Refugees
Unicef	United Nations International Children's Emergency Fund (original acronym retained, but name is now United Nations Children's Fund)
UNIDO	United Nations Industrial Development Organization
UNITEL	Universal Teleservice
UNIVAC	Universal Automatic Computer
Unp	Unnilpentium (element)
Unq	Unnilquadium (element)
UNRWA	United Nations Relief and Works Agency for Palestine Refugees in the Near East
UP	University press (generic)
UP	Upper Peninsula (of Michigan)
UPC	United Presbyterian Church
UPI	United Press International (news service)

UPS	United Parcel Service
UPU	Universal Postal Union (affiliated with the United Nations)
US	United States
USA	United States Army
USA	United States of America
USAAC	United States Army Air Corps
USAAF	United States Army Air Force
USAB	United States Air Base
USACE	United States Army Corps of Engineers
USAF	United States Air Force
USAF	United States Army Forces
USAFA	United States Air Force Academy
USAR	United States Army Reserve
USBE	Universal Serials and Book Exchange (acronym now official name)
USC	United States Code
USCG	United States Coast Guard
USCGA	United States Coast Guard Academy
USDA	United States Department of Agriculture

USF	United States Fleet
USF	United States Forces
USFS	United States Forest Service
USGS	United States Geological Survey
USIA	United States Information Agency
USIS	United States Information Service (name of USIA offices overseas)
USM	United Securities Market (Great Britain)
USMA	United States Military Academy (West Point)
USMC	United States Marine Corps
USN	United States Navy
USNA	United States Naval Academy (Annapolis)
USNB	United States Naval Base
USNR	United States Naval Reserve
USO	United Service Organizations (groups providing assistance, entertainment, etc. to U.S. military personnel)
USPS	United States Postal Service
USS	United States Ship
USS	United States Steamer

USSR	Union of Soviet Socialist Republics
usu.	Usual(ly)
USW	United Steelworkers (of America; union)
UT	Utah (U.S. postal code)
ut dict	As directed (prescription note)
UTLAS	University of Toronto Library Automation System (computer system for libraries)
UTWA	United Textile Workers of America (union)
UTX	United Technologies Corporation
UUA	Unitarian Universalist Association (church)
UV	Ultra-violet
UWA	United Way of America (charity)
UXB	Unexploded bomb

V

V	Five (Roman numeral)
V	Thrift discounted (airfare)
V	Vanadium (element)
v.	Verse
v.	*Versus* (Latin: "against," used in court case citations; see also vs. below)
V	Victory
V	Volt
V	Volume
V1 (or 2)	Vergeltungswaffe-1 or 2 (German: "vengeance bombs"; early missiles used by Germany in last months of World War II)
VA	Veterans Administration (U.S. agency)
VA	Virginia (U.S. postal code)

V & A	Victoria & Albert Museum (London, England)
VAD	Voluntary Aid Detachment (World War I nursing organization in Great Britain)
var.	Variant
VAT	Value added tax (type of sales tax)
vb.	Verb
VC	Victoria Cross (British military decoration)
VC	Vietcong
VCR	Video cassette recorder
VD	Venereal disease
VDU	Visual display unit
VE (Day)	Victory in Europe (World War II)
VEEP	Vice-President
VF	Vertical file
VHC	Vertical hold control (on a television set)
VHF	Very high frequency
VHS	Video Home System (trademark)
VI	Six (Roman numeral)
vi	Verb intransitive

VI	Virgin Islands of the United States (U.S. postal code)
VII	Seven (Roman numeral)
VIII	Eight (Roman numeral)
VIP	Very important person
VISTA	Volunteers in Service to America (Great Society agency)
viz.	*Videlicet* (Latin: "namely")
V-J (Day)	Victory (over) Japan (World War II)
VMD	Doctor of Veterinary Medicine (academic degree)
Vn	Night/off peak thrift discounted (airfare)
VN	Visiting nurse
VO	Very old (liquor ranking)
VOA	Voice of America
vol.	Volume
VOP	Very old pale (brandy rating)
VP	Vice-President
VPL	Visible panty line
VR	Victoria Regina (Queen Victoria of Great Britain)

VRI	Victoria Regina et Imperatrix (Victoria, Queen of Great Britain and Empress of India)
VRM	Variable rate mortgage
vs.	*Versus* (Latin: "against"; see also v. above)
VS	Very superior or special (brandy rating)
VSO	Very superior or special old (brandy rating)
VSO	Voluntary service overseas
VSOP	Very superior or special old pale (brandy rating)
vt	Verb transitive
VT	Vermont (U.S. postal code)
VVA	Vietnam Veterans of America
VVO	Very very old (brandy rating)
VVSO	Very very superior or special old (brandy rating)
VVSOP	Very very superior or special old pale (brandy rating)
VW	Volkswagen (German car)

W

W	Coach economy premium (airfare)
W	Watt
W	Wednesday
W	Wide or width
W	Win(s) (sports abbreviation)
W	Wolfram (element, tungsten)
1-W	Draft classification: conscientious objector performing alternate service
4-W	Draft classification: conscientious objector who has completed alternate service
WA	Washington State (U.S. postal code)
WAAC	Women's Army Auxiliary Corps of the U.S. (later WAC, see below)
WAAF	Women's Auxiliary Air Force (British)

WAC	Women's Army Corps of the U.S.
WASP	White Anglo-Saxon Protestant
WAVES	Women Accepted for Volunteer Emergency Service (U.S. Naval Women's Reserve)
WB	*World Book* (publication)
WB/FP	Wood-burning fireplace
WC	Water closet (British term)
WCC	World Council of Churches
WCTU	Women's Christian Temperance Union (anti-alcohol group)
4WD	Four wheel drive
Wed.	Wednesday
WHO	World Health Organization (affiliated with the United Nations)
WI	Wisconsin (U.S. postal code)
WI	Women's Institute (Great Britain)
WIPO	World Intellectual Property Organization (promotes copyright protection, etc.; affiliated with the United Nations)
WJC	World Jewish Congress
WLB	*Wilson Library Bulletin* (publication)

WLN	Western (formerly Washington) Library Network
WMO	World Meteorological Organization (affiliated with the United Nations)
WNW	West-northwest
WP	Word processing
WP	Working paper
WPA	Works Progress Administration (New Deal agency, later called Works Projects Administration; provided employment through a variety of activities and projects; defunct)
WPC	Woman police constable (Great Britain)
WPI	Wholesale Price Index
WPM	Words per minute
WPPSS	Washington Public Power Supply System
WRAC	Women's Royal Army Corps (Great Britain)
WRAF	Women's Royal Air Force (Great Britain)
WRENS	Women's Royal Naval Service (Great Britain)
WRVS	Women's Royal Voluntary Service (Great Britain)
WSJ	*Wall Street Journal* (publication)

WSW	West-southwest
WV	West Virginia (U.S. postal code)
WWD	*Women's Wear Daily* (publication)
WW I	World War I
WW II	World War II
WX	Westinghouse Electric Corporation
WY	Wyoming (U.S. postal code)
WYSIWYG	What you see is what you get (i.e., a screen display on a computer terminal and its printed version will be more or less the same)

X	Christ (frequently used as an abbreviation in words, e.g., Xian and Xmas for Christian and Christmas)
X	Ex (frequently used as a kind of shorthand, e.g., Xtra for extra)
X	Experimental (typically used by U.S. military to designate specific vehicles at a test stage, e.g., the X-15 airplane/rocket)
X	MPAA (see above) movie rating; persons under 18 not admitted
X	Ten (Roman numeral)
X	USX Corp. (formerly, United States Steel Corporation)
X (cars)	General Motors Corporation's front wheel drive cars
Xe	Xenon (element)
XL	Extra-large (clothing size)
XON	Exxon Corporation

Y	Coach economy (airfare)
Y	Yttrium (element)
YA	Young adult
Yb	Ytterbium (element)
yd	Yard
yd^2	Square yard
yd^3	Cubic yard
YEG	Edmonton, Alberta airport
YHA	Youth Hostel Association
YMCA	Young Men's Christian Association
YMX	Montreal, Quebec airport
Yn	Night/off peak coach (airfare)
YOW	Ottawa, Ontario airport

YQB	Quebec, Quebec airport
YSJ	Saint John, New Brunswick airport
YT	Yukon Territory (Canada; U.S. postal code)
YTD	Year to date
YTZ	Toronto, Ontario airport
YUL	Montréal, Québec airport
YUPPIE	Young urban professional
YVR	Vancouver, British Columbia airport
YWCA	Young Women's Christian Association
YWE	Halifax, Nova Scotia airport
YWG	Winnipeg, Manitoba airport
YYG	Charlottetown, Prince Edward Island airport

Z

Z	F.W. Woolworth Company
Zech.	Zechariah (book of the Bible)
Zeph.	Zephaniah (book of the Bible)
zip	Zone Improvement Plan (Zip code; U.S. Postal Service)
Zn	Zinc (element)
Zr	Zirconium (element)